The Rhodesia Civil List
1902

The Rhodesia Civil List
1902

JEPPESTOWN

JEPPESTOWN

Also available from Jeppestown Press

Where the Lion Roars: An 1890 African Colonial Cookery Book

The Bulawayo Cookery Book and Household Guide

The Anglo-African Who's Who 1907

Matabeleland and the Victoria Falls

With Captain Stairs to Katanga

The Ghana Cookery Book

Cooking in West Africa

The Imperial African Cookery Book

Five-O'-Clock Tea

Fifty Breakfasts

www.jeppestown.com

THE RHODESIA

CIVIL SERVICE LIST,

1902.

CONTAINING

AN ACCOUNT OF THE SERVICES OF THE OFFICERS IN THE CIVIL
SERVICE OF RHODESIA, TOGETHER WITH THE VARIOUS
ESTABLISHMENTS THROUGHOUT THE
TERRITORY, REGULATIONS,
&c., &c.

———————

Published by authority, from Official Records

BY

ARTHUR H. HOLLAND.

ADMINISTRATOR'S OFFICE.

SALISBURY :
PRINTED BY THE ARGUS PRINTING AND PUBLISHING COMPANY, LIMITED,

———

1902

PREFACE.

Rhodesia owes its name to the Right Honourable C. J. Rhodes, whose fore-sight secured this rich and important State for the British Empire. It extends over 750,000 square miles, an area larger than that of France, Germany, Austria, and Italy together, and comprises all the territory (with the exception of the British Central African Protectorate) in the British sphere of influence between the Transvaal and Bechuanaland on the South, Portuguese East Africa on the East, German East Africa on the North-East, and the Congo Free State on the North and North-West.

It is naturally divided by the Zambesi into Northern and Southern Rhodesia, known until 1896 as Northern and Southern Zambesia.

Southern Rhodesia is the high plateau between the Limpopo and the Zambesi, and comprises the two provinces of Mashonaland and Matabeleland. The white population (1901) is approximately 11,000, or 4,000 for Mashonaland and 7,000 for Matabeleland.

Southern Rhodesia is administered under the Charter of 1889, as amended by Orders in Council of 1894 and 1898.

The capital and seat of government is Salisbury (4,700 feet), which is the chief town of Mashonaland, as Bulawayo (4,400 feet) is of Matabeleland. Municipalities were established at both centres towards the close of 1897. Gwelo and Umtali are next in importance, and townships have also arisen at Victoria, Melsetter, Enkeldoorn, Hartley, Rusapi, Gwanda, and Selukwe.

History.—At the time when more than one European Power was anxious to establish itself in Africa, the British Imperial Parliament could not under-take the vast responsibilities involved in the acquisition of such an extensive territory as that now known as Rhodesia, and had it not been for the formation of the Chartered Company, Matabeleland and Mashonaland would probably have fallen either to one of these Powers or would have become part of the South African Republic. President Kruger, finding himself forestalled in his project of acquiring Bechuanaland, had already sent emissaries to Loben-gula, King of Matabeleland, but was once more anticipated by the action of Mr. Rhodes. Early in 1888, Lobengula entered into a treaty of peace and amity with Great Britain, and Messrs. C. D. Rudd, Rochfort Maguire and F. R. Thompson were sent up to Matabeleland to obtain concessions with a view to the formation of the Chartered Company. The Rudd Concession having been granted by Lobengula (30th October, 1888), Her Majesty's Government was approached and a Royal Charter obtained (29th October, 1889).

The Company having decided, on the advice of Lobengula, to open up Mashonaland first, organised a pioneer expedition under Mr. Frank Johnson (June, 1890) consisting of about 200 Europeans and 150 native labourers. The aim of the expedition was to cut a road 400 miles long from Macloutsie, passing through the south of Matabeleland and terminating at Mount Hampden, in Mashonaland. This was duly accomplished, and having founded Fort Salisbury at a spot 12 miles south-east of Mount Hampden (12th September, 1890), the column was disbanded and immediately set to work prospecting, occupying farms, etc.

Much was done by the Company in the the next four years to develop the country. Mr. A. Colquhoun assumed the administration of Mashonaland in October, 1890, there being then about 1,000 white men in the country. Mining Commissioners had to be appointed, townships laid out, roads constructed to different parts, a postal system inaugurated, and measures taken generally for the settlement of the country. Mr. Colquhoun was succeeded by Dr. L. S. Jameson, who was appointed Chief Magistrate by the High Commissioner in September, 1891. For the protection of the community forts had been built at Tuli, Victoria, Charter, and Salisbury, and a military police force was enrolled. The strength of the force in 1891 reached 650, but was reduced as soon as possible to 140 whites and 15 native police, and a Volunteer Force ("Mashonaland Horse") 500 strong, raised locally by Major Forbes, took its place : the remainder of the settlers forming a burgher force in case of need. The Chartered Company arranged for the extension northwards of the Cape Telegraph and Railway from Mafeking, and the surveys for the Beira Railway, connecting Mashonaland with the East Coast, were begun in 1891. A commission of prominent South African farmers came up in 1891 to look into the agricultural prospects of the country and gave a most satisfactory report, resulting in the organisation of the "Moodie trek" of farmers with their families, which left the Orange Free State in May, 1892, and founded the settlement of Melsetter, in Gazaland, early in 1893.

In 1890 and 1891 it was found to be the intention of a number of Boers from the Transvaal to enter the south-east portion of Matabeleland and occupy it by force. This invasion was averted by the firm attitude of the Company and representations were made to President Kruger by the High Commissioner. Boer farmers were, however, invited to come in and settle peacefully in the country ; they now form the majority in the districts of Charter and Melsetter, and assisted the Company loyally during the native troubles.

The same year the Company found themselves somewhat embarrassed by the action of Mr. Edward Lippert, a Transvaal financier and banker, who obtained from Lobengula a concession to grant land titles in the Company's field of operations. As the Rudd Concession did not formally provide for more than mining rights, it was decided to come to terms with Mr. Lippert and to take over his concession. This was accordingly arranged and the matter received the consent of Lord Knutsford, Her Majesty's Secretary of State, in March, 1892.

Other concessions from numerous chiefs were secured soon after the entrance of the Pioneers to the country, the most important being those from Umtassa (Manicaland), Lewanika (Barotseland), and Gungunhana (Gazaland). In connection with certain of these concessions some friction arose with the Portuguese, resulting in the temporary occupation of Massikessi by the Rhodesians. A *modus vivendi* was, however, arrived at, and the most cordial relations have since prevailed.

The year 1893 was a most eventful one for the pioneer community. The Bechuanaland Railway Company had been formed and work started on the Vryburg-Bulawayo extension ; the first section of the Beira Railway had been opened, a good road made from Salisbury to the railhead, and a telegraph line constructed from Mafeking to Salisbury. A period of steady progress was anticipated. Unfortunately, war with the Matabele was forced on the Company by the action of Lobengula. The duties of maintaining peace and order imposed on them by the Charter were made most difficult by the existence of the Matabele military system, under which the Mashonas were periodically raided, their cattle looted, and men, women and children carried into slavery, thus reducing the Mashona tribes to an abject and impoverished condition. On several occasions white men had been stopped and plundered, but conciliatory measures were always adopted, and this was taken by the Matabele to be a sign of weakness, and the raids, apparently restrained at first by the presence of the whites, began to increase in number and extent.

On 18th July, 1893, a Matabele impi made a raid into Mashonaland, about 300 of their number entering Victoria, where they assegaied certain natives and servants of the Company in the streets of the town. Dr. Jameson ordered the invaders to leave the district, and as they refused to avail themselves of the ample time allowed, he instructed the police to eject them. They fired on the police, but were driven out with a loss of 30, and representations were at once made to Lobengula, as the conduct of this impi was a distinct breach of the concessions granted by him on the strength of which the Company had occupied the country. Lobengula, however, sent a defiant answer to the High Commissioner, Sir H. Loch, refusing to treat with the Company until they should give up to him the Mashona fugitives in Victoria.

The Company then prepared for war, informing the High Commissioner that they did not wish to ask the assistance of her Majesty's Government in dealing with the trouble which had arisen. Repeated attempts at negotiations with Lobengula proved fruitless, as he would neither withdraw his demands nor recall his impi, and finally, the Company's police having been fired upon near Victoria on October 2nd, Dr. Jameson was authorised by the High Commissioner to proceed as he thought best.

On October 5th the Matabele fired on a party of Bechuanaland Border Police, an Imperial force patrolling British territory. The High Commissioner immediately ordered Colonel Goold Adams to occupy Tati with a force of Bechuanaland Border Police and to effect a junction with the Company's column at Tuli, which was about to proceed northwards. Khama, King of Bechuanaland, also sent a force ; but this was turned back by order of Colonel Goold Adams. The main body of the Company's forces, consisting of police, settlers and native allies, under the command of Major P. W. Forbes, accompanied by Dr. Jameson, entered Matabeleland early in October, 1893, being joined there by Mr. Rhodes, who had hurried up from the South.

Decisive engagements occurred at the Shangani River (October 24th) and the Bembesi River (November 1st) in which Lobengula's best regiments were thoroughly beaten. Bulawayo, Lobengula's capital, was burnt by Lobengula's orders and left in our hands (November 4th), while the king himself took to flight towards the Zambesi. Letters were sent after him asking him to come back, and guaranteeing his safety ; but no answer having been received before the two days of grace had expired, Major Forbes was instructed to pursue him. On December 3rd, at a point on the Shangani River, 84 miles N.N.W. of Shiloh, the pursuers came close on Lobengula's track, and a small reconnoitring party under Major Alan Wilson crossed the river, which unfortunately came down in flood and cut them off from their companions. After making a most gallant stand they were overwhelmed by the king's body-guard, who did not leave one alive. A monument has been erected to their memory close to the famous Zimbabye ruins. Owing to the difficulty of moving troops in the rainy season, Major Forbes returned to Bulawayo, while Lobengula and the remnants of his band retired towards the Zambesi. Here they fell a prey to small-pox and fever, and the death of Lobengula brought the war to a finish after five weeks of active operations. The military system of the Matabele being broken and their king being dead, it was hoped that the nation would give up their fierce and warlike habits, and they were allowed to retain their arms and to reoccupy their stronghold in the Matoppos.

Owing to the accusations made against the Company to the effect that it had forced on the war for its own ends, a complete enquiry was held by the Imperial Government, as the outcome of which the Marquis of Ripon, Her Majesty's Secretary of State for the Colonies, stated :—" It has given me sincere satisfaction to find that the result of an enquiry so exhaustive and impartial has been clearly to exonerate Dr. Jameson and the officers of the British South Africa Company generally from the serious charges which have been made against them in connection with these occurrences."

Under the altered circumstances of the country it became necessary to discuss its future Administration with Her Majesty's Government and a new Constitution was agreed upon (Order in Council, 18th July, 1894), the Government of the country being carried on by an Administrator (Dr. L. S. Jameson) and a Council of four, consisting of a Judge (Mr. Justice Vintcent) and three other members (Colonel F. W. Rhodes, D.S.O., Military Member of Council, A. H. F. Duncan, Surveyor-General, and George Pauling, Commissioner of Public Works). The regulations passed by the Administrator in Council were agreed to have the force of law, after approval and promulgation by the High Commissioner.

At the time of framing this Constitution, Mr. Rhodes was most anxious to insert a provision to prevent the imposition of any customs dues on British goods in excess of the rates then in force in the South African Customs Union, which are low rates levied for purposes of government and not for protection or prohibition. His object was to secure the trade of Rhodesia to England for ever at a low tariff rate. Her Majesty's Government did not at that time see their way to adopt this proviso, but the next Cabinet accepted it (Order in Council, 1898), fixing the rate on the basis of the existing Cape tariff. The importance of this tie between the Mother Country and the new territories cannot be over-estimated.

The two years which followed (1894 and 1895) were marked by prosperity and peace. The mining and farming industries were pushed on and the railways and telegraphs extended. With the absorption of Matabeleland and the taking over of the Northern sphere it was considered wise to reorganise the Volunteer Force. At the same time a force of Native Police, consisting entirely of Matabele (mostly from Lobengula's crack regiments) was established, their main duties being to assist Native Commissioners in police and detective work in connection with the natives.

The political disturbances which had long been threatening in the Transvaal culminated in December, 1895, when Dr. Jameson, with a force largely composed of the Company's Police, made an unauthorised incursion into the South African Republic, with a view to assisting the Uitlander population. The result was a fiasco, and Dr. Jameson's force was met and broken up at Doornkop, near Johannesburg, President Kruger handing over his prisoners to the British Government to be dealt with. Dr. Jameson's resignation from the position of Administrator was accepted early in 1896, and the Right Honourable the Earl Grey succeeded him in April of that year.

After these events certain changes in the Constitution were made, providing for closer control of the Administration by the Crown.

The Company's territory, deprived for the time of its police protection owing to the Jameson Raid, was at a disadvantage when a second Matabele war broke out in March, 896 ; but the danger to the whole population was successfully averted by the courageous and self-reliant action of the settlers. The causes of the rising are thought to be as follows :—

First. The incomplete subjugation of the Matabele in 1893.

Second. The inability of a warlike and masterful people to settle down at once under a peaceful regime.

Third. The premature organisation of Native Police, whose actions are said to have been irritating and overbearing.

Fourth. The influence of the priests of the "Mlimo" (the Matabele god), who persuaded the Matabele that the phenomenal combination of physical plagues which fell upon the country at this time were a curse due to the presence of the white man. In the first place a drought of abnormal length and severity had prevailed ; locusts, which do not seem to have troubled the country much for a quarter of a century, appeared in swarms of extraordinary magnitude ; thirdly, rinderpest, a disease hitherto quite unknown in Southern Africa, came down from the North, destroying whole herds of Matabele cattle. The Government determined, in order to check the southward progress of the disease, to establish a clear belt by shooting all the cattle in a certain area. It was difficult for the Matabele to see the wisdom of this measure, and when in addition to these plagues a disease broke out among them from eating rinderpest meat their superstitions were easily worked upon by the native priests. They determined to rid themselves of the whites, and had they combined to attack the towns simultaneously, as it is believed was their original intention, the white population would have been taken unawares; but fortunately the natives had not sufficient self-control to carry out this scheme, and news was brought in from the outlying districts of the brutal and treacherous murders of many isolated individuals and small parties, the number of men, women and children thus massacred amounting in all to 141.

Measures for protecting the community were at once taken. Laagers were formed at Bulawayo and Gwelo, and Major Laing with his small party also went into laager at Belingwe. All white men in the outlying districts were called in. The existing Volunteer Force was expanded into the Bulawayo Field Force, and under the leadership of Colonels W. Napier, J. Spreckley and Hon. Maurice Gifford, Captains Macfarlane, George Grey and F. C. Selous numerous patrols were sent out from Bulawayo in various directions, and they were successful in bringing in small parties of refugees.

The salvation of the settlers lay in the want of concerted action among the natives, whose neglect to block the Mangwe Pass, the only line of communication

with the South, is almost inexplicable.   To keep this pass open a chain of forts
was built along the Mangwe road.

The great danger to the Bulawayo laager was that the Matoppo and
Umgusa rebels might combine and rush the town, but on April 25th Captain
Macfarlane engaged the enemy at the Umgusa, and defeated them so heavily
as to remove all cause for anxiety.

The difficulty of sending food supplies, forage, arms, ammunition and
reinforcements to a population of 4,000, in a town 587 miles away from its railway base and besieged by 15,000 natives, was very considerably augmented by
the fact of the war coming directly after rinderpest.   This had not only
destroyed the main source of the fresh meat and milk supply, on which the
country depended, but also the transport system.   A mule transport service
had to be organised at a moment's notice.   Owing to the famine in the
Protectorate, grain, which was requisite for these mules, was unobtainable from
Mafeking to Bulawayo, and the commissariat difficulty was, thereby, much
increased.

It was necessary to follow up with vigour Captain Macfarlane's victory ;
the settlers, however, were not strong enough to accomplish this, and the
Imperial Government issued instructions for the inhabitants to wait for reinforcements.   Colonel Plumer, with a force of Volunteers, left Mafeking on April
12th and reached Bulawayo at the end of May, after a brilliant engagement at
the Khami.   Simultaneously, a column raised in Salisbury under Colonel Beal,
and accompanied by Mr. Rhodes, left for the relief of Bulawayo.   Colonel
Napier went out to meet them, defeating the rebels at Thabas Induna, and
Colonel Beal, after a successful action at Mavene, joined Napier's force and
proceeded to Bulawayo, bringing in quantities of captured stock.

Sir R. Martin arrived in Bulawayo on May 21st, and took over command
of military operations until the arrival of General Sir F. Carrington
on June 3rd.   Two columns under Plumer and Macfarlane were sent
out North and South, and a third was on the point of starting when an impi
appeared at the Umgusa, six miles out of Bulawayo.   Colonels Spreckley and
Beal immediately moved against them and inflicted heavy loss on the enemy.
Spreckley's column then set out as originally intended, and the three columns
swept the country of rebels.   Colonel Plumer stormed and carried the stronghold of Thabas Imamba, where he made important captures of prisoners, grain
and cattle, and recovered a quantity of loot taken from murdered settlers.

The country was now practically free of rebels, except the Matoppos, where
they occupied positions which were considered impregnable.   The Matoppos
consist of rugged granite kopjes extending over a region 60 miles in length by
10 to 20 miles broad, and form a difficult piece of country to clear, owing to the
existence of innumerable caves and boulders which hid the enemy.   The operations conducted against the rebels were successful, but extremely tedious.   Mr.
Rhodes, therefore, determined to open negotiations, which he accordingly did
on the 21st August, by going five miles into the hills accompanied by three
unarmed men, and holding an indaba with the rebel chiefs.   To further allay
the suspicions of the natives he moved his camp, which was quite unprotected
by any military force, to a spot close to the rebel stronghold, where he remained
for two months, reassuring and conferring with the natives.   On October 13th
the Administrator had an official indaba with the Matabele chiefs, and received
their formal promises of submission.   Colonel Plumer's column was disbanded

on the 22nd of the same month, many of its members remaining in the country as settlers.

Long before the restoration of peace to Matabeleland trouble had appeared in Mashonaland. Envoys from the Matabele are known to have been sent to the Charter and Hartley districts, in order to work on the superstitions of the Mashonas and to excite them to rise in rebellion. The first warning of a rising, which broke out in June, 1896, was the news of a series of murders similar to those in Matabeleland. Nearly all the available men and arms had gone in the Salisbury column to the relief of Matabeleland, so there was little to be done but to form laagers in the principal centres and to maintain a defensive attitude until the arrival of reinforcements.

Mr. Justice Vintcent was at the head of affairs in Salisbury, and immediately organised a defence committee and called in all the population to laager. The number of able-bodied men was 350, with 60 police; about 250 guns were collected and issued to them.

One of the first events which followed was the stirring episode of the rescue of a party of twelve, including three women, who gathered at the Alice Mine, in the Mazoe district, 27 miles from Salisbury. In order to telegraph for assistance two of their number heroically volunteered to go to the telegraph office. They were successful in sending their message, but were killed in trying to regain the laager. On receiving the telegram Inspector Judson left Salisbury with five men, but found the situation at the laager so desperate that he sent a message to Salisbury to say that it would require 40 men and a Maxim to effect a rescue, as the whole Mazoe Valley was lined with natives some 1,000 strong. Captain Nesbitt, who had gone out with 12 men to reinforce Inspector Judson's patrol, received the message and determined, notwithstanding the smallness of his force, to push on. He succeeded in bringing out the party and for this deed was awarded the Victoria Cross. The return journey was accomplished under heavy fire, all concerned displaying much courage.

A small body of Volunteers from Natal, under Captain Taylor, who were at Charter on their way to Matabeleland, returned to Salisbury on the outbreak of hostilities, as did Colonel Beal's column of the Rhodesia Horse Volunteers, which was then at Bulawayo. These latter were accompanied by 100 men under Major Watts D.A.A.G., and 75 men of Grey's Scouts under Captain White. They arrived at Salisbury on the 16th and 17th July, after which the laager was broken up and martial law revoked.

Large patrols were now sent out to commence offensive operations against the natives, pending the arrival of 380 regular troops under Colonel Alderson, which had been sent through Beira from Natal. They reached Salisbury on the 9th of August, having relieved Umtali en route. Colonel Alderson remained five months in the country, and, although much hampered by shortness of supplies, he effected the capture of the important chief Makoni and the destruction of many rebel kraals and attacked and defeated Matshayangombi, who may be said to have been the leader of this rebellion. It was considered that this had practically brought the trouble to an end and that the settlement of the country might be left to Sir Richard Martin aided by a police force of 580 whites and 100 native contingent. The Imperial troops accordingly left Rhodesia on November 29th, 1896.

It soon became evident that the natives were far from being subdued, and that Matshayangombi was not long in recovering from the defeat inflicted on him. He proceeded to reoccupy his strongholds, where he gathered rebels from all quarters, and, being joined by Mkwati and Kagubi, the two chief priests of the Mlimo, was able to arouse fresh courage in the Mashona tribes.

The rebellion thus entered on a fresh stage. Frequent attempts were made to induce the rebels to surrender, and it was decided to adopt and maintain harassing tactics until the end of the rainy season, when more active steps could be taken. In April, Colonel de Moleyns commenced vigorous operations with a successful attack on the Magwendi rebels, followed up by the defeat of Kunzi and Mashanganyika. The Mashonaland forces having been strengthened by a detachment of Hussars and police from Matabeleland, the country about Salisbury, Umtali, and Charter was cleared of rebels and a well-organised attack made on Matshayangombi (24th July, 1897), when the latter was shot in attempting to escape, his stronghold destroyed, and his followers dispersed and disheartened. It was decided to be unnecessary to retain the services of the Hussars after September. This date practically marks the close of the campaign, and the police having reached their full complement, the volunteers were disbanded and returned, some to their farms and others to the mining centres. The energetic and self-reliant conduct of the settlers during the war and many instances of bravery, individual and general, form a record in the history of the new country of which it may well be proud.

It was decided by the Company to adopt a policy of compensation to settlers for direct losses incurred during the rebellion, this being the first time any Administration in South Africa has awarded compensation for injuries inflicted on its subjects in native warfare. The Compensation Courts paid out £253,500 in Matabeleland, and the awards in Mashonaland brought up the sum to £360,000.

During the period occupied by the war the attention of the Government was not only devoted to meeting questions of defence and transport. It was felt necessary to reorganise the Civil Service of the country and to establish it on a permanent basis. This work was carried out by Mr. W. H. Milton, who was transferred to Rhodesia from the Cape Colony Civil Service in July, 1896, as Chief Secretary to the Administrator (Earl Grey) whom he succeeded in July, 1897.

The next problem to be met was the settlement of the native question, and in this respect the first thing to do was to relieve the famine which had broken out among the natives. In order to check the mortality from this cause, the Company lost no time in importing grain to feed their late antagonists. 1,000,000 pounds of grain were accordingly brought up to Bulawayo and distributed among the starving people of Matabeleland at a time when transport entailed a cost of 1s. a pound. This meant a cost of £50,000 from the railhead alone, to which must be added the railway charges and initial cost.

The Government proceeded to hold indabas with the rebel chiefs, at which their grievances and wishes were heard, and the methods proposed by the Administration for their future government explained to them. These seemed to be quite understood by the chiefs, and have answered satisfactorily up to the present time (1902). The system then adopted of maintaining salaried indunas has worked very well, especially with the Matabele, who being of Zulu origin, have always been used to organised government by important chiefs, who are in turn responsible to a central authority. The indunas have justified the confidence placed in them, the young indunas in particular being quick to grasp what is required of them. The Mashonas have never been one great nation like the Matabele; but they have grown accustomed to the rules of tribal government as laid down in the Southern Rhodesia Order in Council, 1898. An indirect incentive to induce the natives to work was supplied by informing them that it was intended to impose a hut-tax, on the basis of 10s. a hut, at some date not far distant ; also to recognise their traditional custom of lobola. This is the original Zulu marriage custom under which the man pays a certain number of cattle to the father of his spouse. The effect of this system is to stimulate the young men to earn money with/which to pay for their marriage, and also to check immorality among the natives, which is found to prevail where the custom has lapsed.

In both provinces the natives have settled down quietly on the large reserves set apart for them from some of the best agricultural ground in Rhodesia. In Matabeleland alone 5,000,000 acres are devoted to this purpose, an area far more than sufficient for their present needs, while in Mashonaland up to the present over 8,000,000 acres have already been allotted and further reserves are in course of demarcation.

With regard to acquisition of property by the natives, it must be remembered that in the time of Lobengula no individual Matabele had any right to own cattle, which were all the property of the King, and before the company came to check the Matabele raids the Mashonas were never allowed to possess their stock in peace. Thus it was not till the settlement of the country by the Chartered Company that the individual native could enjoy the rights of property. They have had little difficulty in reaching a condition of great prosperity, as the following table, illustrating their material progress, will show.

	1897-1898.	1898-1899.	1899-1900.	1900-1901.
CATTLE—				
Mashonaland -	9,295	17,379	27,682	30,853
Matabeleland -	4,688	6,751	8,973	13,073
Total -	13,983	24,130	36,655	43,926
SHEEP AND GOATS—				
Mashonaland -	64,522	79,920	117,980	129,043
Matabeleland -	22,186	36,307	58,242	89,654
Total -	86,708	116,227	176,222	218,697
ACREAGE UNDER CULTIVATION—				
Mashonaland -	226,591	410,581	388,888	499,041
Matabeleland -	101,994	121,967	127,083	134,803
Total -	328,585	532,548	515,971	633,844

INCREASE BETWEEN 1897 AND 1901.

Cattle, 13,983 to 43,926 ... ... over 200 per cent.
Sheep and Goats, 86,708 to 218,697 ... ... over 150 ,,
Acreage under cultivation, 328,585 to 633,844 nearly 100 per cent.

Superstition and the natural indolence of the native, are ever the greatest obstacles to progress towards civilisation, and cannot be removed at one blow. The bad plight in which the prophecies of the "Mlimo" left the natives, added to the downfall of such important personages as Kagubi, the chief prophet, and Nyanda, the prophetess, was not without its influence ; and though the natives are occasionaly found to indulge in practices due to their belief in witchcraft, these are only isolated cases, which are always kept as secret as possible from the Government, who discourage such actions by every means in their power.

In 1899 an event of great interest took place in the establishment of a Legislative Council for Southern Rhodesia, under the Southern Rhodesia Order in Council of 1898, which embodied to a large extent the proposals of the Board of Directors to meet the wishes of the settlers with regard to obtaining a voice in the government of the country. This was accomplished by including an elective element in the Council together with a number of members nominated by the Company sufficient to ensure it a majority so long as it remains responsible for the finances of the country. The first elections were held in April, 1899, and the first session opened in May, since when a considerable amount of legislative work has been accomplished.

Transvaal War.—At the end of 1899, war having broken out between Great Britain and the South African Republic, Rhodesia was not behind other dependencies in coming to the assistance of the Imperial cause both by raising local forces and in other ways made necessary by the peculiar circumstances of the country.

In August 1899 Colonel Baden-Powell was given the supreme command of all forces in Rhodesia and the Protectorate, collectively called the Rhodesia Regiment. After the investment of Mafeking, the command of the northern wing devolved on Lieut.-Colonel Plumer who was stationed at Tuli, which he established as his base. By the interruption of communication with the South on the declaration of war (11th October) his force was completely cut off from the Cape ports on which he naturally depended. His only line of communication and supply lay, therefore, through Rhodesia, as follows :—To Bulawayo, 200 miles and thence to Salisbury, 280 miles of ox transport ; thence to the Portuguese port of Beira, 380 miles of rail. A further difficulty existed in the fact that it was not until several months later that the Portuguese Government decided to allow munitions of war to pass over the Beira line. Colonel Plumer thus found himself not only responsible for the protection of the loyal natives of Bechuanaland and the defence of the Rhodesian frontier, but he had also to do his best to aid Colonel Baden-Powell and the besieged town of Mafeking, without having the necessary artillery, reserves of ammunition and equipment, or even money to pay his column. All these were forthwith provided by the Company, who placed their stores at his disposal and assisted him to the utmost of their power. As many of the British South Africa Police as could possibly be spared were sent to augment his force, which at first consisted of 450 men– mostly Colonials– soon to be reinforced by a squadron of Southern Rhodesia Volunteers under Colonel Spreckley, C.M.G. The Southern Rhodesia Volunteers were originally called out for the purpose of defending the Rhodesia border, but they were also subsequently employed outside the Company's dominions in the re-establishment of communication with the South and the relief of Mafeking. All the railway employés between Palapye and Lobatsi were, on the outbreak of the war, enrolled as the Railway Troop of the Southern Rhodesia Volunteers, their duties being to guard and repair the line, while the Engineers' staff of the Rhodesia Railways at Bulawayo were set to work to fit out armoured engines and trucks to be used in excursions on the railways through the Protectorate.

Colonel Plumer disposed the greater portion of his force along the Crocodile River which he guarded against the Boers until December ; skirmishes between the patrols on either side being of frequent occurrence.

In the meantime a force of Southern Rhodesia Volunteers, under Colonel Holdsworth, had moved steadily down from Bulawayo to Mochudi, in the Protectorate, repairing the railway and telegraph lines as they advanced.   As it was now evident that the Boers had abandoned their intention of entering Rhodesia, Colonel Plumer felt he could devote his whole resources to the assistance of Mafeking, and moved the bulk of his troops from Tuli to a point on the railway 22 miles north of Mochudi.   He now assumed direct command of the troops in the Protectorate, numbering over 1,000, composed mostly of British South Africa Company Police and volunteers from Rhodesia.   The work of repairing the line was then continued southwards with a rapidity and courage which reflect great credit on the Railway Troop.   Part of the repairs (replacing the bridge over the Metsimashwani River) was done under actual fire from the Boer guns, which could not be answered till the arrival of two guns, one from Tuli and one from Bulawayo.   Colonel Plumer was then able not only to defend himself, but on occasion to assume the offensive.   The Boers having evacuated their position at Crocodile Pools and retired towards Mafeking, the Rhodesian forces pushed on to Lobatsi, and thence southwards to a position 30 miles N.W. of Mafeking, where the Boer forces were now concentrated.   For the next two months the Rhodesian forces moved about the neighbourhood of Mafeking, directing their efforts to getting in supplies and getting out non-combatants from the beleaguered town, thus easing the strain on the commissariat, 1,200 natives being in this manner brought out and fed. This was the extent of what Colonel Plumer could at this time undertake single handed towards the relief of Mafeking, as he had nothing to equal the Boer artillery and no possibility of getting reinforcements or support beyond another 200 men with a 2·5 gun which arrived from Rhodesia, and as he had, moreover, to bear in mind that on his force alone the defence of Rhodesia depended.

On May 14th a detachment of the Royal Canadian Artillery and 100 dismounted men of the Queensland Mounted Infantry, with four guns, arrived from the North, whence they had been sent forward with the greatest rapidity. This was the first detachment of the Rhodesia Field Force under General Sir Frederick Carrington, which had in the meantime been landed at Beira.

Men, horses, equipment and stores had to be brought up over the Beira railway, which had been since the outbreak of hostilities in process of con-version to the broad gauge, and which was at the same time the sole channel of supply for the whole of Southern Rhodesia.   This line runs through the low and unhealthy Portuguese territory, unsuitable for any other mode of trans-port, and had the railway not been available, Rhodesia would have been in an awkward predicament when the Bulawayo line was in the possession of the Boers.   The success with which all obstacles were overcome was largely due to the energy of Mr. A. L. Lawley (manager for Pauling & Co., the railway contractors).   Headquarters were established at Marandellas, stores erected along the line of march and troops expedited through Rhodesia to the front by the Administration, which acted throughout as agents for the Imperial Government in the matter of supplying equipment, provisions and transport for the force during its progress through the country.

* To understand the strain on the resources of Rhodesia as regards wagon transport, it must be borne in mind that at the time this was required by the troops, the population of Bulawayo had to be supplied through Salisbury, instead of by rail through Mafeking as usual, and though a certain number of

transport oxen had been imported into Rhodesia since the extermination of the cattle by rinderpest, scarcity in this respect still prevailed. The fact of supplying His Majesty's troops at the seat of war with draught oxen thus made the necessary transport of supplies for Rhodesia very difficult and expensive.

Being now certain of reinforcements in case of the Boer invasion or native complications, Colonel Plumer started at once and effected a junction with the column, which had been working its way from the South for the relief of Mafeking. On May 16th the Boers were defeated 10 miles from Mafeking, and on May 17th the combined columns marched into the town. On May 19th the column moved North to cover the repairs to the railway, which were completed on May 22nd, thus bringing Mafeking in touch w.th Bulawayo.

The latter work of the Rhodesia Regiment belongs to the history of the campaign in the Transvaal.

The part taken by Rhodesians in the war was not limited to the defence of its own frontier and the relief of Mafeking. At Colonel Plumer's urgent request a large number of the Company's Police, of whom no less than 450 were serving under him in the Protectorate before the relief of Mafeking, continued to form part of the column which proceeded to carry on active operations in the Transvaal. Numbers of Rhodesians enrolled in the various Colonial Corps in the Cape Colony and Natal, approximately 17 per cent. of the whole European population, or 20 per cent. of the adult male population having been on active service since the beginning of the war. Leave of absence was granted to as many members of the public service as could possibly be spared to proceed to the front, although the work of the remainder was made considerably heavier through the great pressure thrown on the Administration by the duty of protecting and supplying a territory suddenly cut off from its military and commercial base, and, in addition, by the necessity of aiding the Imperial authorities with every means at their disposal.

Not only did the settlers rise to the occasion, but the attitude of the natives throughout the war was most satisfactory. They were pleased to have the state of affairs explained to them and remained quiet and loyal through a period which might well have been expected to unsettle their minds.

Development of the Country.—Notwithstanding the natural difficulties of developing a new country, so large and remote—thrown back as it was by successive wars and the ravages of rinderpest—the progress accomplished during the 11 years of the history of Rhodesia has been far from inconsiderable.

Railways.—Two railway systems have been introduced into Rhodesia:—

First. The Main Trunk Line, being the Cape Government system, continued *via* Mafeking northward through Bechuanaland into Rhodesia. This forms part of the Cape to Cairo railway, a section of which, from its connection with the Cape portion at Ramaquabane, was completed as far as Bulawayo in October, 1897. The formal opening of this section at Bulawayo on November 4th was an occasion of great rejoicing, coming as it did on the close of the Matabele rebellion, and after many privations and much patient waiting on the part of the settlers. It was attended by Her Majesty's High Commissioner, the Governor of Natal, Members of the English Parliament (from both Houses), and other guests from England and America, besides about 200 representatives from all parts of South Africa and a number of native indunas and chiefs.

Another section, 160 miles long, is being pushed on from Bulawayo in the direction of the coalfields at Wankies and the Victoria Falls. The gauge (3ft. 6in.) is that adopted throughout South Africa and Egypt. It was this uniformity which enabled Mr. Rhodes to help Lord Kitchener at an important crisis in the Soudan campaign, by lending him four engines which had been designed for use in Rhodesia.

Second. The East Coast Line. A light railway from Beira to Umtali was opened in January, 1898, and was at once widened to the 3ft. 6in. gauge, this being accomplished in May, 1900, in the face of floods and other complications presented by the unusual congestion on the line, due to the requirements of the military authorities, and the needs of the civil population of Rhodesia, including the mining companies. The 3ft. 6in. line from Umtali to Salisbury had been opened in May 1899 Salisbury being thus connected with Beira, 382 miles distant.

In addition to these lines a 3ft. 6in. line, 200 miles in length, has been constructed from Salisbury to Gwelo to meet a line 100 miles long from Bulawayo, a continuous overland route being thus established between Beira and Capetown. A line of the same gauge is being taken in hand from Bulawayo to the Gwanda district, besides which a light railway is in course of construction from Salisbury to the Ayrshire Mine, in the Lomagundi district.

Telegraphs.—There are under the Administration nearly 3,000 miles of telegraph lines, the whole system embracing 81 offices. The main line extends from Mafeking in the Cape Colony through Salisbury to Umtali, from which point the Transcontinental Telegraph, part of the "Cape to Cairo" project, extends through North-East Rhodesia to Lake Tanganyika. By agreement with the German Government this line has been carried on in the direction of British East Africa and is now about 100 miles north of Abercorn.

Mines.—Hitherto, owing to the other demands on the railways, in the form chiefly of transport of fresh permanent way, not much facility has been offered for bringing up heavy mining material. Nevertheless, steady progress has been made, as may be seen from the following table :—

	ozs.	dwts.
Output up to 31st December, 1898 ...	24,555	13
Output for 1899	65,303	13
Output for 1900	91,940	8
Output for 1901	172,061	9
Total	353,861	3

During the Transvaal War the work of the mines never stood still. Most of the large companies had laid in a stock of supplies : but when these threatened to give out, the Government came to the assistance of the mining community, helping to bring up mining requisites and foodstuffs. The closing of the mines would, it was felt, be a serious misfortune to the country, as not only would a large number of men be thrown out of work and local stores forced to close, but the effect on the native mind would have been deplorable in view of the efforts that were being made in certain quarters to persuade the natives that the white men were deserting the country.

The coal deposits at Wankies, now being developed, have proved very rich, being in the opinion of experts better in quality than any South African coal and almost equal to a similar class of Welsh steam coal. Promising coal finds have been made in the Victoria, Tuli, Lomagundi and Sebungwe districts, and rich copper mines have been discovered. Silver, plumbago, lead, tin, iron, antimony, slate, salt, asbestos, arsenic and kieselguhr are also known to exist.

Agriculture.—Agriculture has made steady progress throughout Rhodesia; more work has naturally been done where a market exists than where this has not yet been provided by the development of the local mines. The farming industry includes the breeding of cattle, horses, sheep, pigs, goats, ostriches and poultry; the cultivation of cereals, vegetables, and European fruits, all of which appear to flourish in Rhodesia. Many vegetable products, peculiar to sub-tropical regions, are indigenous and should therefore thrive under cultivation; among these are rice, tobacco, indiarubber and cotton.

Since the blow dealt by rinderpest to the stock farmers, Government has been importing breeding cattle in large numbers, allowing farmers to have them on easy terms. Seeds of various kinds have also been provided.

Education.—The number of children locally educated shows the genuine nature of the colonisation of the country. The Government in 1900-1 spent the sum of £4,000 on educational grants under the provisions of the Educational Ordinance, 1899.

NORTHERN RHODESIA.

Northern Rhodesia was originally brought into notice by the explorations of Dr. Livingstone. In 1889 it was brought under the provisions of the African Order in Council of that date, and is now administered under the Barotziland—North-Western Rhodesia Order in Council of 1899, and the North-Eastern Rhodesia Order in Council of 1900.

North-Western Rhodesia (Barotseland) has as Administrator, Mr. R. T. Coryndon, who resides at Lealui. The most important tribe is the Barotse, to which the other tribes are subject. With Lewanika, the intelligent and powerful chief of the Barotse, most friendly relations have always prevailed. He sought British protection on his own initiative, and in 1890 granted the Company mineral and trading concessions over the whole of his dominions, and he has subsequently agreed to its civil administration by the Company.

North-Eastern Rhodesia is administered by Mr. R. Codrington from Fort Jameson, which is the capital. The white population is about 120, and the Districts and Sub-districts into which the country is divided are under the care of Collectors and Sub-collectors, assisted by a force of 210 civil police, recruited from various African tribes.

Northern Rhodesia is for the greater part a continuation of the high and healthy South African plateau which extends from the Karoo through Southern Rhodesia and north of the Zambesi. Its altitude makes up for its proximity to the Equator, the highlands being temperate and fertile like those of the Shiré, and apparently favourable for raising cattle and sheep, and for growing cereals and all kinds of European fruits and vegetables. The settlers are for the most part employed in agriculture, stock breeding and trading, the country not having yet been extensively prospected for minerals. Gold has been found, though it has not been ascertained whether it is in payable quantities; iron is known to the natives, who make many articles from it; coal exists at Lake Nyassa, and should be valuable in working the steamers there; while rich discoveries of copper have been made and are now being exploited in the Hook of the Kafue. The rubber trade is the most important at present, and ivory is also exported ; but coffee, palm oil and fibre promise to become of importance, and the native tobacco is said to be of an excellent quality.

History. — Up to the time of the acquisition of Northern Rhodesia by the Company, the work of civilisation was carried on by various missions and a Company known as the African Lakes Company, was employed in developing the country. Both this Company and the missions were much hampered in their work and their existence imperilled by the Arab slave raids which were of continual occurrence ; and as at the time it was not apparent that the Imperial Government intended to administer any part of this territory itself, the Chartered Company decided that it was advisable, for the protection of British interests and for the maintenance of law and order, to buy out the African Lakes Company and to take the country north of the Zambesi under its own influence. Early in 1891 the Imperial Government extended the field of the Company's operations so as to include the whole of the British sphere north of the Zambesi, except Nyassaland, now known as the British Central African Protectorate, which they took under their own administration. Mr. (now Sir Harry) Johnston was appointed Imperial Commissioner for Nyassaland in March 1891 and was permitted by Her Majesty's Government to act as Administrator over the rest of the Company's northern territories. It was arranged for the British South Africa Company to defray the expense of administering the whole sphere under annual subsidies of £10,000 to £17,500, which were almost entirely expended on the Nyassaland Protectorate, principally in maintaining the police force necessary to check the raids of the Arab slave traders. In 1894 the Company's total expenditure for this purpose amounted to £75,000, and in this year a new arrangement was made with the Imperial Government, under which the Chartered Company undertook to assume direct administration of the whole of Northern Zambesia. Major P. W. Forbes went up at midsummer, 1895, as the company's first Administrator ; but, his health failing in 1897, he was relieved by Captain Daly.

In 1896, Major Forbes reported that the Arab slave raids were practically at an end, but that a menace to the country still existed in the power of the Awemba, a tribe of unparalleled cruelty and ferocity inhabiting the south of the Tanganyika plateau in North-Eastern Rhodesia, their custom being to raid other tribes and to co-operate with the Arab slave traders. In September, 1897, a large number of Arabs, acting in concert with the Awemba, came into collision with the Company's officials and were thoroughly defeated, the power of the Arabs being thus completely broken. Of the Arab chiefs responsible for these raids not more than three remain in the country : they carry on small trading operations, and have hardly any following or influence, and are on good terms with the Government. The Awemba have ceased to be a source of dread since the death of their great chief Mwamba in 1898, and since the occupation of their country by the British South Africa Company (October, 1898) not one case of mutilation or human sacrifice, hitherto of shockingly frequent occurrence, has taken place.

The predominant people in the south of North-Eastern Rhodesia are the Angoni, under M'pesini, whose depredations caused considerable trouble for some years. In December, 1897, a serious rising took place, which was effectually quelled and M'pesini's authority reduced.

Thus, in a few years, the settlement of the greater portion of the company's northern territories was brought about.

A. H. H.

CALENDAR

JANUARY, 31 Days.				FEBRUARY, 28 Days.				MARCH, 31 Days.		
D. of M.	D. of W.			D. of M.	D. of W.			D. of M.	D. of W.	
1	W	New Year's Day.		1	S	Criminal Sessions. Bul.		1	S	Civil Term Salisbury
2	Th			2	Sun	Sexagesima.		2	Sun	3 in Lent. [begins.
3	F			3	M			3	M	
4	S			4	Tu			4	Tu	
5	Sun	2 after Christmas.		5	W			5	W	
6	M	Epiphany.		6	Th			6	Th	
7	Tu			7	F			7	F	
8	W			8	S			8	S	
9	Th			9	Sun	Quinquagesima.		9	Sun	4 in Lent.
10	F			10	M			10	M	
11	S			11	Tu			11	Tu	
12	Sun	1 after Epiphany.		12	W			12	W	
13	M			13	Th			13	Th	
14	Tu			14	F			14	F	
15	W			15	S	{ Civil Term Bul. begins		15	S	Civil Term Bul. ends.
16	Th					{ Prov. ay, Salisbury.		16	Sun	5 in Lent.
17	F			16	Sun	Quadragesima.		17	M	St. Patrick's Day.
18	S			17	M			18	Tu	
19	Sun	2 after Epiphany.		18	Tu			19	W	
20	M			19	W			20	Th	
21	Tu	Prov. Day, Bul.		20	Th	Crim. Ses., Salisbury.		21	F	
22	W			21	F			22	S	
23	Th			22	S			23	Sun	Palm Sunday
24	F			23	Sun	2 in Lent.		24	M	
25	S			24	M			25	Tu	
26	Sun	Septuagesima.		25	Tu			26	W	
27	M			26	W			27	Th	
28	Tu			27	Th			28	F	Good Friday.
29	W			28	F			29	S	Civil Term S'bury ends.
30	Th							30	Sun	Easter Day.
31	F							31	M	Easter Monday.

APRIL, 30 Days.				MAY, 31 Days.				JUNE, 30 Days.		
D. of M.	D. of W.			D. of M.	D. of W.			D. of M.	D. of W.	
1	·u			1	Th			1	Sun	1 after Trinity.
2	W			2	F			2	M	
3	Th			3	S			3	Tu	
4	F			4	Sun	5 after Easter.		4	W	
5	S			5	M	Crim. Ses., Bulawayo.		5	Th	
6	Sun	1 after Easter.		6	Tu			6	F	
7	M			7	W			7	S	
8	Tu			8	Th	Ascension Day.		8	Sun	2 after Trinity.
9	W			9	F			9	M	
10	Th			10	S			10	Tu	
11	F			11	Sun	After Ascension.		11	W	
12	S			12	M			12	Th	
13	Sun	2 after Easter.		13	Tu			13	F	
14	M			14	W			14	S	Civil Term Bul. ends.
15	Tu			15	Th	Civil Term Bul. begins.		15	Sun	3 after Trinity.
16	W			16	F			16	M	Prov. Day, Salisbury.
17	Th			17	S			17	Tu	
18	F			18	Sun	Whit Sunday.		18	W	
19	S			19	M	Whit Monday.		19	Th	
20	Sun	3 after Easter.		20	Tu			20	F	Crim. Ses., Salisbury.
21	M			21	W			21	S	
22	Tu			22	Th			22	Sun	4 after Trinity.
23	W	St. George's Day.		23	F			23	M	
24	Th			24	S	Victoria Day.		24	Tu	
25	F			25	Sun	Trinity Sunday.		25	W	
26	S			26	M			26	Th	
27	Sun	4 after Easter.		27	Tu			27	F	
28	M			28	W			28	S	
29	Tu			29	Th			29	Sun	5 after Trinity.
30	W			30	F			30	M	
				31	S					

Days in Italics are Government Holidays.

FOR 1902.

JULY, 31 Days | AUGUST, 31 Days. | SEPTEMBER, 30 Days.

D.of M.	D.of W.		D.of M.	D.of W.		D.of M.	D.of W.	
1	Tu	Civil term Salisbury	1	F		1	M	Civil Term Salisbury
2	W	[begins.	2	S		2	Tu	[begins
3	Th		3	Sun	10 after Trinity.	3	W	
4	F		4	M		4	Th	
5	S		5	Tu	Civil Term Bul. ends.	5	F	
6	Sun	6 after Trinity.	6	W	Crim. Ses., Bulawayo.	6	S	
7	M		7	Th		7	Sun	15 after Trinity.
8	Tu		8	F		8	M	
9	W		9	S		9	Tu	
10	Th		10	Sun	11 after Trinity.	10	W	
11	F		11	M		11	Th	
12	S		12	Tu		12	F	Occupation Day,
13	Sun	7 after Trinity.	13	W		13	S	Mashonaland.
14	M		14	Th		14	Sun	16 after Trinity.
15	Tu	Civil term Bul. begins.	15	F	Prov. Day, Salisbury.	15	M	
16	W		16	S		16	Tu	
17	Th		17	Sun	12 after Trinity.	17	W	
18	F		18	M	Prov. Day, Bulawayo.	18	Th	
19	S		19	Tu		19	F	
20	Sun	8 after Trinity.	20	W	Crim. Ses., Salisbury.	20	S	
21	M		21	Th		21	Sun	17 after Trinity.
22	Tu		22	F		22	M	
23	W		23	S		23	Tu	
24	Th		24	Sun	13 after Trinity.	24	W	
25	F		25	M		25	Th	
26	S		26	Tu		26	F	
27	Sun	9 after Trinity.	27	W		27	S	
28	M		28	Th		28	Sun	18 after Trinity.
29	Tu		29	F		29	M	
30	W		30	S		30	Tu	Civil Term S'bury ends.
31	Th	Civil term S'bury ends.	31	Sun	14 after Trinity.			

OCTOBER, 31 Days. | NOVEMBER, 30 Days. | DECEMBER, 31 Days.

D.of M.	D.of W.		D.of M.	D.of W.		D.of M.	D.of W.	
1	W				{ Crim. Ses., Bul.	1	M	
2	Th		1	S	{ Civil Term S'bury beg's	2	Tu	
3	F		2	Sun	23 after Trinity.	3	W	
4	S		3	M		4	Th	Shangani Day.
5	Sun	19 after Trinity.	4	Tu	Occupation Day, Mata-	5	F	
6	M		5	W	beleland.	6	S	
7	Tu		6	Th		7	Sun	2 in Advent.
8	W		7	F		8	M	
9	Th		8	S		9	Tu	
10	F		9	Sun	24 after Trinity. King's	10	W	
11	S		10	M	[Birthday.	11	Th	
12	Sun	20 after Trinity.	11	Tu		12	F	
13	M		12	W		13	S	
14	Tu		13	Th		14	Sun	3 in Advent.
15	W		14	F		15	M	Civil Term Bul. ends.
16	Th		15	S	Civil Term Bul. begins.	16	Tu	
17	F		16	Sun	25 after Trinity.	17	W	
18	S		17	M		18	Th	
19	Sun	21 after Trinity.	18	Tu	Civil Term S'bury ends.	19	F	
20	M		19	W		20	S	
21	Tu		20	Th	Crim. Ses., Salisbury.	21	Sun	4 in Advent.
22	W		21	F		22	M	
23	Th		22	S		23	Tu	
24	F		23	Sun	26 after Trinity.	24	W	}
25	S		24	M		25	Th	Christmas Day
26	Sun	22 after Trinity.	25	Tu		26	F	Public Holiday.
27	M		26	W		27	S	
28	Tu		27	Th		28	Sun	1 after Christmas.
29	W		28	F		29	M	
30	Th	Prov. Day, Bulawayo.	29	S		30	Tu	
31	F		30	Sun	1 in Advent.	31	W	

Days in Italics are Government Holiday

ALPHABETICAL INDEX

OF THE

Civil Establishment Returns.

Adcock, W. H.	18	Blanckenberg, R. A.		10
Addison, F. H.	23	Blanckenberg, W. R.		18
Ade, E. G.	12	Boardman, C. H. C.		17
Amos, T. N.	21	Boardman, J.		13
Anderson, J.	14	Bodle, Lt.-Col. W.		23
Ashmead, H.	21	Bolling, E. T.		21
Aston, E. J. S.	16	Bowden, Capt. F. L.		23
Atherstone, W. J.	22	Bowen, G. J.		21
Austin, Miss B. de Bruno	22	Brailsford, E. A. L.		18
		Breen, M.		20
		Brereton, H. J. K.		20
Bagshawe, A. C.	21	Briggs, A. E.		59
Bagshawe, B. F.	21	Briggs, C. W.		21
Bain, A.	18	Brooks, J. A.		13
Baker, A. L.	19	Broun, F. S.		21
Balch, H. E.	13	Brown, A. H.		10
Barbour, W. S.	19	Buller, Hon. W. Yarde		23
Barnard, M. W.	16	Burgess, R. G.		26
Barnes, F. R.	12	Burrow, R.		25
Barrett, C. H.	11	Buxton, E. A.		11
Barrie, N.	12	Byas, A. W.		11
Barry, A. M. Harte	23	Byers, B. H.		14
Baxter, E. C.	11	Byron, F. R.		15
Baxter, J. R. B.	11			
Bayley, C.	17			
Bayne, L. L.	11	Cameron,		22
Beadle, A. W.	11	Campbell, A. A.		16
Beaty-Pownall, E. G.	21	Campbell, C. M.		21
Beaufort, the Hon. Mr. Justice		Campbell, Miss E. M. S.		14
Leicester P.	25	Campbell, F. C.		16
Bell, A.	11	Carbutt, C. L.		17
Bell, A. B.	11	Carden, Capt. J.		23
Benzies, W. R.	11	Carson, E. Hope		10
Berry, T.	11	Cartwright, O.		14
Bibra, L. F.	15	Cary, C. W.		19
Biddulph, W. T.	18	Cashel, R.		23
Bill, D.	14	Castens, H. H.		10
Birch, C. de K.	22	Cazalet, Capt. A. P. L.		23
Birch. J. de Gray	20	Chapman, H.		23
Blackwell, C.	10	Chataway, N. H.		17
Blackwell, J. S.	11	Chawner, Capt. H.		23
Blanckenberg, C. H.	59	Chesnaye, C. P.		25

Chester-Master, Colonel R.	23	Downing, A. W. ... 14
Clark, T. C. ...	25	Drew, A. ... 15
Clarke, F. J. ...	16	Drury, Capt. G. V. ... 23
Clarke, T. R. ...	14	Duff, C. E. ... 10
Clayton, E. T. ...	23	Dunbar, G. D. ... 17
Cloete, H. A. ...	11	Dunbar, S. T. ... 17
Cloete, S. V. ...	17	Dunford, J. ... 14
Codrington, R. ...	25	Duthie, G. ... 11
Cole, W. ...	22	Dutton, P. E. ... 14
Coleman, J. W. ...	12	
Collard, C. T. A. ...	25	Earl, H. E. ... 13
Collyer, J. ...	13	Eardley-Mare, E. J. ... 15
Colquhoun, W. N. ...	10	Easom, E. ... 25
Coltsman-Cronin, T. J. ...	19	Eastwood, F. E. ... 23
Cooke, C. B. ...	17	Eaton, W. M. ... 14
Cooke, G. ...	22	Eddie, N. L. K. ... 22
Cookson, P. C. ...	26	Edge, A. E. ... 20
Coope, J. C. Jesser ...	21	Edwards, W. ... 15
Cordner, H. ...	17	Eickhoff, C. ... 14
Cornwell, R. de Vere ...	14	Elliot, F. G. ... 17
Cox, H. R. ...	26	Elliot, H. A. ... 16
Coxhead, J. C. C. ...	25	Elliot, W. ... 14
Crago, T. ...	13	Ellis, R. ... 12
Crake, E. A. ...	11	Elworthy, Miss H. G. ... 13
Craven, P. E. ...	11	Emerton, A. F. ... 12
Cresswell, A. T. ...	13	Evans, R. N. ... 12
Crewe, C. ...	18	Evered, H. R. ... 13
Critchley-Salmonson, G. L. B.	21	Everett, Major R. H. ... 23
Croad, H. ...	25	Eyre, G. H. ... 12
Crowther, A. E. ...	25	
Cumming, G. W. ...	22	Fairbairn, K. B ... 18
		Farmaner, G. W. ... 18
Dale, A. ...	16	Farmery, E. A. ... 22
Dally, W. J. ...	13	Farquaharson, P. C. ... 21
de Jong, J. ...	26	Farrer, W. E. ... 17
Dennison, F. W. ...	13	Ferguson, D. W. ... 25
De Smidt, J. P. L. ...	19	Fernside, J. D. F. ... 22
De Stadler, P. J. ...	12	Fielde, W. R. ... 10
Devine, W. A. ...	12	Fisher, F. ... 12
Devitt, C. ...	13	Fisher, J. T. ... 16
Dickson, A. M. ...	20	Fleming, Dr. A. M., C.M.G. 14, 23
Dilworth, W. C. ...	22	Fleming, C. D. ... 21
Dobson, J. ...	13	Fleming, G. N. ... 21
Donald, W. M. ...	17	Fletcher, C. M. ... 18
Dooner, H. B. ...	14	Flint, Lt.-Col. J. ... 23
Douglas, J. C. E. ...	21	Forbes, J. H. ... 26
Douslin, H. B. ...	21	Forbes, Major P. W. ... 24

Forrestall, P. ...	...	16	Harvey, P. G. R.	...	21
Fox, F. Wilson	...	10	Hawksley, J. A. D.	...	21
Freeman, D. C.	...	13	Healy, J. J. ...	...	20
Fuller, H. G. ...	...	16	Hearn, H. W.	...	19
Fuller, Capt. J. W.	...	20	Helm, A. G. ...	...	21
Fynn, C. G. ...	...	16	Helm, B. A. Mc. M.	...	21
Fynn, H. C. K.	...	15	Henman, R. A.	...	13
Fynn, M. D. ...	...	15	Hett, C. ...	...	13
Fynn, P. D. L.	...	17	Hewat, J. W. ...	...	12
			Heyman, A. A. I.	...	21
Gardiner, C. J. R.	...	19	Hinds, C. F. ...	...	22
Gardner, T. Scott	...	14	Hinds G. ...	...	10
Gilbert, P. F. ...	...	19	Hiscock, W. J.	...	21
Gillespie, D. ...	...	12	Hoal, E. ...	...	19
Gilliland, G. S. S.	...	12	Hodson, F. A. ...	...	23
Gilson, Capt. C. H.	...	23	Hole, H. Marshall	...	18
Glanville, T. G.	...	13	Holland, A. H.	...	10
Goldschmidt, H. T.	...	11	Holland, A. T.	...	15
Goode, R. A. J.	...	25	Holloway, A. E.	...	12
Gordon, J. F. ...	...	17	Hone, A. R. ...	...	21
Gorman, J. J. ...	...	22	Hone, P. F. ...	...	21
Gosling, Major A. V.	...	23	Honey, W. H. L.	...	18
Gowers, W. F. ...	...	17	Hook, W. D. ...	...	15
Granger, C. F.	...	18	Hopper, Major H. H.	...	23
Gray, C. E., M.R.C.V.S.	...	22	Hopgood, C. J. S.	...	21
Greenway, K. ...	...	23	Howell, C. H. ...	... 15. 23
Greer, H. F. ...	...	16	Hubbard, A. T.	...	12
Greer, J. L. ...	...	26	Hughes, J. C. ...	...	25
Greer, S. W. ...	...	19	Hulley, T. B. ...	... 15, 19
Griffin, T. ...	...	21	Hunt, A. C. ...	...	13
Griffith, H. F.	...	17	Hunt, Miss A. H.	...	12
Griffith, R. H. ...	...	23	Hunt, J. G. ...	...	12
Grimaldi, A. J.	...	21	Hunt, P. G. ...	...	13
Gwynne, P. ...	...	23	Huntly, G. M.	...	19
			Hurrell, W. C.	...	22
Hall, P. E. ...	...	25	Hyland, J. ...	...	19
Hancock, W. P. T.	...	13	Hyland, P. ...	...	19
Harbord, R. A.	...	11			
Hardy, H. H. C.	...	23	Illes, J. F. H. ...	...	14
Harley, E. C. ...	...	12	Ingham, J. S. ...	...	23
Harper, H. A. ...	...	21			
Harper, R. B. ...	...	18	Jackson, H. M. G.	...	16
Harpur, J. ...	...	14	Jackson, J.	...	19
Harrington, H. T.	...	26	Jackson, S. N. G.	...	16
Harris, G. T. J.	...	18	James, G. H. ...	...	21
Harris, T. H. ...	...	13	Jarvis, E. M., M.R.C.V.S.	...	22
Harvey, Miss A. E.	...	13	Jearey, J. G. ...	...	10

d.

Jennings, W. J. ...	13
Johnstone, B. B. ...	26
Jones, A. L. ...	16
Jones, E. A. A. ...	26
Jones, F. E. F. ...	26
Jones, L. G. ...	11
Jones, N. S. ...	14
Judson, D. ...	12
Kearney, F. X. ...	22
Keen, H. R. H. ...	13
Kennedy, J. H. ...	18
Kennedy, P. J. ...	12
Kennelly, W. P. ...	25
Kenny, E. T. ...	15
King, G. J. ...	18
King, W. A. ...	16
Kinghorn, W. S. ...	25
Kirby, A. C. ...	18
Kirschbaum, G. M. ...	18
Kleinschmidt, Miss J. M. ...	13
Kotze, J. G. ...	17
Krienke, R. ...	12
Krige, W. A. ...	11
Laessoe, H. H. de ...	17
Laing, W. T. ...	17
Lambert, A. J. ...	13
Lanning, R. ...	16
Lapham, T. U. ...	12
Laurie, C. G. ...	21
Lawlor, E. J. ...	18
Lawson, W. ...	14
Leahy, K. A. ...	12
Lee, F. H. S. ...	22
Lee, Hans ...	22
Leigh-Lye, F. M. ...	19
Le Sueur, G. W. ...	18
Lewis, D. M. ...	20
Lever, G. M. E. ...	26
Lidderdale, R. H. ...	23
Lingard, M. A. ...	22
Lister, H. C. ...	14
Longden, W. M. ...	19
Low, W ...	17
Lyons, G. G. P. ...	26
Macey, W. H. ...	13
Macgregor, J. ...	14
Macglashan, N. ...	21
Macdougall, J. W. ...	20
MacIntosh, R. ...	14
Macqueen, Capt. W. J. ...	23
Madgen, L. H. ...	14
Makunga, J. C. ...	16
Mann, W. ...	13
Marshall. Miss A. ...	12
Marshall, H. C. ...	26
Martin, A. ...	11
Martin, D. A. ...	25
Masterman, T. S. ...	24
Masterson, L. C. ...	23
Mathews, C. J. ...	22
Matthews, A. H. ...	22
Maughan, J. ...	20
McCulloch, G. H. ...	18
McDonald, D. ...	10
McDonald, R. S. ...	26
McGibbony, J. ...	13
McIlwaine, H. ...	18
McIlwaine, R. ...	17
McKinnon, C. ...	26
McNeil, J. ...	26
Medcalf, F. G. ...	13
Mee, E. B. O. ...	13
Melland, F. H. ...	26
Mellor, S. P. ...	18
Melville, J. H. ...	21
Mercer, E. B. S. ...	18
Meredith, L. C. ...	15
Miles, H. P. ...	19
Millar, E. W. ...	14
Miller, A. C. R. ...	26
Milton, J. ...	18
Milton, His Honour W. H.	10
Money, Capt. C. F. L. ...	23
Monro, C. F. H. ...	21
Monro, Capt. C. F. L. ...	23
Montagu, E. W. S. ...	21
Moodie, D. H. ...	16
Moore, W. H. ...	24
Morris, E. W. ...	15
Morris. H. G. ...	22
Morris, S. F. ...	11

Moss, G. E. ...	...	11
Muller, L.	...	11
Mundell, M. H. G.	...	24
Murray, W. E.	...	23
Myburgh, A. de M.	...	24
Myburgh, P. D.	...	18
Myburgh, R. A.	...	11
Myburgh, R. H.	...	19
Nanson, H. J. ...	...	20
Nauhaus, C. F. W.	...	19
Nell, A.	...	18
Nesbitt, Capt. R.C., V.C.	... 15,	23
Nevitt, J. H. ...	...	13
Newman, L.	...	12
Newnham, A. H.	...	17
Newton, O. J. ...	...	13
Norris, S. B. ...	...	21
Nunan, D.	...	12
O'Connor, J. T.	...	13
Ogilvie, O. H. ...	...	21
O'Leary, D. M.	...	13
Oliphant, S. J.	...	21
Olive, W.	...	11
O'Reilly, R.	...	19
Orpen, C. E.	...	22
Orpen, J. M.	...	22
Orpen, W. H. ...	...	17
Osborne, H. J.	...	13
Owen, A. D.	...	15
Parkin, H. C. ...	...	25
Peacock, K. D.	...	18
Peel, A. J. R. ...	...	18
Pett, A. G.	...	17
Phelps, C. H. ...	...	14
Phillips, D. T. ...	...	14
Phipps, A. B. ...	...	23
Pidcock, C. A. ...	...	18
Pidcock, G. H.	... 15,	19
Posselt, J. W. ...	...	16
Powell, J. P. A.	...	12
Power, J. R. ...	...	13
Powys-Jones, Ll.	...	18
Prew, A. W. B.	...	12
Quin, H. C.	...	19

Raikes, T. A. ...	...	15
Rangeley, H. ...	...	18
Rankine, A. B.	...	10
Read, J.	...	12
Redfern, A. W.	...	18
Redmond, V. ...	...	13
Reid, J. L.	...	25
Reid, J. W.	...	17
Reid, V. B.	...	26
Rice, F.	...	20
Richards, J. A.	...	26
Rivers, C. H. ...	...	21
Roberts, G.	...	13
Roberts, L. F. H.	...	19
Robertson, Jas.	...	10
Robinson, H. ...	...	20
Robinson, L. G.	...	16
Rose, A. E.	...	12
Ross, A. R.	...	15
Rothwell, S. R.	...	26
Russell, A.	...	12
Rusell, M.	...	21
Rust, F.	...	13
Sandilands, P.	...	19
Sandilands, Mrs. J. H.	...	19
Savage, W. E. M.	...	25
Sawerthal, H. G. E. J. E. ...		22
Scanlen, the Hon. Sir Thomas		
C., K.C.M.G.	...	17
Scott, W. E. E.	...	15
Scully, E. de L.	...	11
Selby, P. H. ...	...	25
Sellars, A.	...	13
Selmes, H. P. ...	...	21
Shand, W. R. ...	...	19
Sharp, E. C. ...	...	18
Sheehan, F. G.	...	12
Shekleton, J. E.	...	26
Short, C.	...	17
Short, G.	...	11
Sinclair, A.	...	13
Sinclair, J. M., M.R.C.V.S.		22
Slocock, C. E.		21
Slowey, W. J.	...	14
Smith, E. D. ...	...	14
Smith, F. J. M.	...	18

Smith, F. W. ...	20	Timmler, C. H.	...	25
Smith, Mrs. M.	19	Tobilcock, T. H. M.	...	12
Smith, P. G. ...	19	Tomlinson, A. J.	...	23
Smith, T.	19	Tomlinson, G., M.R.C.V.S.		22
Smith, W. ...	12	Tonge, A. R. ...	...	18
Smith-Wright, E. H.	17	Townsend, A. H.	...	13
Smyth, H. K. ...	14	Townsend, E. R.	...	22
Snelling, F. R.	12	Townsend, T. W. F.	...	21
Spain, W. S. ...	23	Tredgold, C. H.	...	18
Speight, A. E. ...	11	Trott, W. H. ...	...	13
Spillane, J. C. ...	25	Truan, E. ...	...	13
Spreckley, H. U.	21	Tucker, W. W.	...	18
Sprigg, W. P. ...	11	Tyler, A. E. ...	...	13
Standing, F. ...	11			
Stapleton, G. F.	11	Vance, R. H. C	...	11
Stephenson, J. E.	26	Varley, H. C. ...	...	11
Stevens, C. ...	26	Vincent, the Hon. Mr. Jus-		
Stevens, J. A. ...	11	tice, J. ...	...	18
Stewart, D. W.	20	Wadeson, T. J.	...	12
Stewart, E. H. J.	21	Wakeford, R. J.	...	13
Stewart, W. D.	17	Walker, H. S. ...	...	12
Stidolph, A. ...	22	Watermeyer, the Hon. Mr.		
St. John, W. E.	23	Justice J. P. F.	...	18
Stops, G. ...	23	Watkins, H. B.	...	14
Straker, Major M.	23	Watson, Blair....	...	26
Strickland, A. ...	22	Webber, O. W.	...	13
Stuart, C. T. ...	16	Weinand, C. E. P.	...	22
Stuart, P. A. ...	16	Westley, C. H.	...	12
Sybray, J. ...	11	West-Sheane, J. H.	...	26
Symons, S. M.	11	Wetherall, G. J.	...	13
		White, S. G. R.	...	21
Taberer, H. M.	15	Williams, A. G.	...	11
Taberer, W. S.	15	Williams, G. H. P.	...	23
Tagart, E. S. B.	25	Williams, J. H.	...	16
Tait, J. ...	24	Williams, M. J.	...	14
Taylor, E. D. ...	16	Williams, S. E.	...	26
Taylor, H. J. ...	16	Willis, H. G. ...	...	25
Taylor, W. M. ...	15	Wilmont, H. ...	...	12
Tennant, J. D.	22	Wilson, E. ...	...	14
Thebault, J. ...	12	Wolhuter, G. H.	...	14
Theron, H. F. ...	12	Wood, R. H. ...	...	15
Thian, A. ...	12	Wragg, W. S. ...	...	15
Thomas, C. C. ...	11			
Thomas, F. R.	19	Yates, F. A. ...	...	19
Thomas, T. M.	16	Yates, F. Y. ...	...	22
Thomas, W. E.	16	Young, A. ...	...	15
Tilney, W. A. ...	17	Young, R. ...	...	26

THE SOUTHERN RHODESIA

CIVIL SERVICE LIST.

Part 1.

SECRETARIES OF STATE FOR THE COLONIES, 1887—1901.

1887. Jan. 12. Right Hon. Sir Henry Thurston Holland, Bart., G.C.M.G., afterwards Viscount Knutsford.

1892. Aug. 18. The Marquess of Ripon, K.G.

1895. June 28. The Rt. Hon. Joseph Chamberlain, M.P.

COLONIAL OFFICE, DOWNING STREET.

Secretary of State :—The Right Hon. JOSEPH CHAMBERLAIN, M.P.
 Private Secretary :—Lord MONK BRETTON.
Parliamentary Under Secretary :—The Earl of ONSLOW, G.C.M.G.
Permanent Under Secretary :—Sir M. F. OMMANNEY, K.C.M.G.
 Assistant Under Secretary (for South African Affairs) :—F. GRAHAM, C.B.
South African Department :— H. W. JUST, C.M.G., H. C. M. LAMBERT, G. E. A. GRINDLE, G. G. ROBINSON, D. O. MALCOLM.

THE HIGH COMMISSIONER.

On the 20th August, 1889, a Commission was issued under the Royal Sign Manual and Signet, appointing the Governor and Commander-in-Chief or other officer for the time being administering the Government of the Colony of the Cape of Good Hope to be, during pleasure, High Commissioner for South Africa.

Extract from Colonial Office List, 1901.

The High Commissioner was till 1899, charged with the conduct of British relations with the South African Republic (Transvaal), and the Orange Free State, as well as those with native states and tribes outside the colonies of the Cape and Natal, including Swaziland, which was administered by the Government of the South African Republic under the Convention of 1894. The High Commissioner is also Governor of Basutoland, and supervises the affairs of the Bechuanaland Protectorate, and he exercises the control provided by Order in Council over the administration of the British South African Company in Southern Rhodesia (*i.e.*, South of the Zambesi). The Southern Rhodesia Order in Council, 1898, provides for a control by the High Commissioner over legislation, important appointments, and native affairs in Rhodesia, and for the appointment of an Imperial Resident Commissioner, who is the subordinate of the High Commissioner, and of an Imperial Commandant of the armed forces, the control of which was taken away from the Company after Dr. Jameson's raid into the Transvaal, and placed under the High Commissioner. It has now been arranged that the office of High Commissioner shall be held with that of Governor of the Transvaal, and Sir A. Milner will fill both offices.

On the 10th October, 1878, Letters Patent were isssed under the Great Seal of the United Kingdom, empowering the High Commissioner for the time being to grant local rank to Imperal military officers.

HIGH COMMISSIONERS, 1889—1901.

1889. Sir H. B. Loch, G.C.B,. G.C.M.G.
         (Created Baron Loch, 1895).
1895. The Right Hon. Sir Hercules, G. R. Robinson, Bart., G.C.M.G.
         (Created Baron Rosemead, 1896).
1897. Sir Alfred Milner, G.C.B., G.C.M.G.
         (Created Baron Milner, 1901).

ACTING HIGH COMMISSIONERS, 1889—1901.

1889. Lieut.-General H. A. Smyth, C.M.G.
1891 and 1892. Lieut.-General W. G. Cameron, C.B.
1894. General Sir William G. Cameron, K.C.B.
1895 and 1896. Lieut.-General W. H. Goodenough, C.B.
1897. Lieut-General Sir William H. Goodenough, K.C.B.
1898. Major-General George Cox.
1898 and 1899. Lieut.-General Sir W. F. Butler.
1901. Lord Kitchener, G.C.B., G.C.M.G., General Commanding-in-Chief H.M's. Forces in South Africa.

GOVERNMENT HOUSE, JOHANNESBURG.

High Commissioner :—Lord Milner, G.C.B., G.C.M.G.
    Private Secretary :—M. S. O. Walrond, C.M.G.
Imperial Secretary and Accountant :—F. Perry.

Military Secretary :—Major the Hon. W. LAMBTON, D.S.O.
Chief Clerk :—C. H. Rodwell.
    Assistant Accountant :—E. B. Burley (lent from Colonial Office).
    Clerks :—E. H. R. Garthorne, E. W. Neal, E. Cohen.
    Shorthand Writer :—Miss Hanbury.
    Typists :—Miss Kent, Miss Dickson.
Secretary to Governor of Orange River Colony :—Lord BASIL BLACKWOOD.

Part II.
ADMINISTRATION.

1. The Company* shall have and may exercise the general administration of affairs within the limits of this † Order, in accordance with the terms of the Charter and any Charter amending the same or Supplementary thereto and the provisions of the Order in Council of 20th October, 1898.

2. (*a*) The Company* may exercise such administration by one or more Administrators, and under him, or them, by such other officers as may from time to time be necessary, and may from time to time, with the approval of a Secretary of State, determine the number of Administrators.

(*b*) The Company* with the approval of a Secretary of State, may from time to time assign the local limits of the province within which an Administrator shall act.

(*c*) Whenever there is more than one Administrator the Company, with the approval of a Secretary of State, shall determine the precedence of the several Administrators.

3. The Company* shall appoint the Administrator or Administrators and shall pay his or their salaries and the salaries of such officers as may be required for the administration of Southern Rhodesia : but shall obtain the approval of a Secretary of State before appointing any person to the office of Administrator. The salary of an Administrator shall be fixed by the Company,* with the approval of a Secretary of State, and shall not be increased or diminished without his approval. An Administrator may be removed or suspended from office by a Secretary of State or by the Company* with the approval of a Secretary of State

4. (*a*) An Administrator shall hold office, unless sooner removed, for three years from the date at which he enters upon the duties of his office : and with the approval of a Secretary of State may from time to time be re-appointed for a further term of three years. At the end of any such term an Administrator shall continue in office until re-appointed or until his successor is appointed.

(*b*) If at the end of any such term, or if on a vacancy in the office the Company* does not within three months thereafter, with the approval of a Secretary of State, re-appoint an Administrator or appoint his successor, a Secretary of State may appoint some person to be Administrator.

---

    * The Company is the British South Africa Company
    † Order in Council of 20th October, 1898,

5. (a) The Company,* with the approval of a Secretary of State, may appoint some person to act as Administrator in the event of the death, removal, resignation, absence from Southern Rhodesia, incapacity or suspension of an Administrator. A Secretary of State or the Company* with the approval of a Secretary of State may remove or suspend an acting Administrator.

(b) The precedence, powers, and duties of an Acting Administrator shall, unless othewise determined by the Company,* with the approval of a Secretary of State, be the same as that of the Administrator in whose place he is acting.

(c) When there is no Administrator or Acting Administrator appointed by the Companay* to any Province capable of discharging the duties of the office the Administrator or Acting Administrator of the other Province of Southern Rhodesia, or, if there shall be more than one other Province, the senior of such Administrators or Acting Administrators, or if there shall be no such Administrator or Acting Administrator in Southern Rhodesia capable of discharging the duties of the office, the Senior Member of the Executive Council other than the Resident Commissioner shall act as Administrator for the Province in which there is such vacancy.

THE ADMINISTRATOR.

The office of "Administrator" first came into existence by Section 8 of the Order in Council of 1894, prior to which the Representative of the Chartered Company in Mashonaland was designated Chief Magistrate.

The following is the list of Chief Magistrates, Administrators, etc. :—

Chief Magistrates.

1891 [24th July.] A. R. Colquhoun (Acting).

1891 [18th September] Dr. Leander Starr Jameson, C.B., M.D.

1893 [7th October.] A. H. F. Duncan (Acting).

Administrators.

1894 [10th September.] Dr. Leander Starr Jameson, C.B., M.D.

1896 [2nd April.] The Right Hon. Earl Grey.

1898 [5th December.] Administrator of Mashonaland and Senior Administrator of Southern Rhodesia, W. H. Milton, C.M.G.

1898 [5th December.] Administrator of Matabeleland, Captain the Hon. A. Lawley. Resigned on appointment as Governor West Australia, March, 1901.

Acting Administrators.

1894 [2nd October.] Colonel Francis Rhodes.

1895. His Honour Judge Vincent.

1897 [July.] W. H. Milton.

1898 [5th December.] The Hon. Sir Thomas C. Scanlen, K.C.M.G.

1899 [20th June.] Captain the Hon. A. Lawley (Mashonaland).

---

* The Company is the British South Africa Company.

EXECUTIVE COUNCIL.

The Executive Council consists of the Senior Administrator, the Resident Commissioner, every Administrator other than the Senior Administrator, and not less than four members appointed by the Company with the approval of a Secretary of State. A member of the said Council shall hold office for three years, unless sooner removed by the Company, with the like approval, but shall be eligible for re-appointment.

The Company, with the approval of a Secretary of State, shall, subject to the provisions of the Order in Council of 20th October, 1898, determine the precedence of members of the Executive Council.

The Administrator shall preside at the meetings of the Executive Council. In his absence, the Administrator next to him in order of precedence who is present, or if no Administrator is present, such other member of the Executive Council as the Senior Administrator shall designate in writing, shall preside at the Meetings of the Council.

The Executive Council shall meet whenever summoned by the Administrator at such time and place as shall be specified in the summons.

The Administrator shall on the request of any other Administrator or of the Resident Commissioner immediately summon the said Council.

Three members exclusive of the Resident Commissioner shall form a quorum.

An Administrator shall take the advice of the Executive Council upon all matters of importance affecting the administration of affairs within the limits of the Province to which he has been appointed, except in cases which are too urgent to admit of their advice being taken. In all such urgent cases the Executive Council shall as soon as possible be summoned and acquainted with the action taken and the reason therefor.

An Administrator may act contrary to the advice of the Executive Council. but in every such case he shall report the matter forthwith to the Company, with the reasons for his action. In every such case any member of the Council who dissents may require that the reasons for his dissent be recorded and transmitted to the Company. The Company may reverse any action of an Administrator whether taken with, or without, or against, the advice of the Executive Council.

The Members of the Executive Council are :—

President :

William Henry Milton, C.M.G., Senior Administrator, &c., &c., &c., 5th December, 1898.

Members :

Lieutenant Colonel Sir Marshal James Clarke, K.C.M.G., Resident Commissioner, &c., &c., &c.
John Gilbert Kotze (Attorney General), 9th August, 1900.

Sir Thomas Scanlen, K.C.M.G. (Legal Adviser), 20th December, 1898.
Joseph Millerd Orpen (Surveyor General), 20th December, 1898.
Townshend Griffin (Commissioner of Mines and Works), 20th December, 1898.

Clerk :

Jas. Robertson.

Part III.

RESIDENT COMMISSIONER.

The Secretary of State may appoint an officer who shall reside within Southern Rhodesia, and who shall be called the Resident Commissioner.

The Resident Commissioner shall be paid out of money provided by Parliament such salary and allowance as a Secretary of State, with the concurrence of the Treasury, may determine.

The Resident Commissioner shall be *ex-officio* a member of the Executive and Legislative Councils, and shall be entitled to be present at any meeting of either Council, and at any meeting of any Committee thereof, and shall be entitled to speak but not to vote at any such meeting.

The Resident Commissioner shall make a report to the High Commissioner upon every Ordinance submitted for his assent, and upon all appointments submitted for his approval, and shall, as occasion may require, fully inform the High Commissioner upon all matters of importance arising within the limits of the Order in Council of 20th October, 1898.

The Resident Commissioner takes precedence next after the Administrator.

Every Administrator shall supply or cause to be supplied to the Resident Commissioner, by such Officer and at such place as may be desired, all such information and all such documents of whatever nature having reference to the administration or the officers and servants of the Company as the Resident Commissioner may at any time require, and shall furnish true copies of any such documents at any time if requested by the Resident Commissioner so to do.

Resident Commissioner : Lieut.-Col. Sir Marshal J. Clarke, K.C.M.G.

Secretary : C. Douglas Jones.

Part IV.

LEGISLATIVE COUNCIL.

The Legislative Council of the Territory was constituted by Section 17, Sub-section 1, of the Order in Council of 20th October, 1898.

It consists of the Administrator or Administrators for the time being, the Resident Commissioner, and nine other members, of whom five shall be nominated by the British South Africa Company, with the approval of a Secretary of State, and four who shall be elected by the registered voters in the Territory.

For the purpose of electing the members of the Legislative Council, the Territory is divided into two provinces, returning two members for each province, elected for a period of three years. The provinces and the members at present representing them are :—

Mashonaland.	*Matabeleland*
William Paterson Grimmer.	Elliot St. Maurice Hutchinson,
Colonel Raleigh Grey, C.M.G.	Dr. Hans Sauer,

The nominated canditates who take precedence over the elected candidates are :—

John Gilbert Kotze, *Attorney-General.*

Joseph Millerd Orpen, *Surveyor-General.*

Townshend Griffin, *Commissioner of Mines and Works.*

Herbert Hayton Castens, *Chief Secretary.*

Clarkson Henry Tredgold, *Solicitor_General.*

James Hutchinson Kennedy, *Master of the High Court (during the abscence of* Mr. Griffin).

Clerk of Council, James Robertson.

The Senior Administrator is President of the Legislative Council, and in his absence, the Administrator next to him in order of precedence who is present, or, if there be no Administrator present such other member of the Council as may be appointed in writing by the Administrator, shall preside at the meetings of the Council, and may take part in any debate and in the event of any equality of votes the Administrator or other presiding member shall have a casting as well as a deliberate vote. No person shall be qualified to be elected a member who is an infant or is not a British subject by birth or naturalization, or who has within five years before his election, or since his election, been convicted of any crime, and sentenced to imprisonment with hard labour without the option of a fine, or to any greater punishment, and has not received a free pardon, or has, within or during the time aforesaid, surrendered his estate as insolvent, or made a composition or arrangement with his creditors. Provided that where a person is disqualified by having surrendered his estate as insolvent, or made a composition or arrangement with his creditors, the disqualification shall cease in case of insolvency, when the debtor has obtained his rehabilitation or paid his debts in full.

SESSIONS OF THE LEGISLATIVE COUNCIL.

COUNCIL.	Whether opened or prorogued.	Session.		
		1st	2nd	3rd
First ...	Opened ...	1899 May 15	1900 March 21	1901 July 3
	Prorogued ...	June 19	March 31	August 3

ORDINANCES, 1901.

1.—Indemnity Ordinance.
2.—Native Marriages Ordinance.
3.—War Material Export Prohibition Ordinance.
4.—Peace Preservation Ordinance.
5.—Masters and Servants Ordinance.
6.—Licence and Stamp Ordinance.

7.—Animals Diseases Ordinance.
8.—Gold Trade Ordinance.
9.—Telegraph Protection Ordinance.
10.—Wearing of Uniforms Ordinance.
11.—Lo Magundi Railway Ordinance.
12.—Hut Tax Ordinance.
13.—Customs Tariff Amendment Ordinance.
14.—Excise Duty and Management Ordinance.
15.—Settlement of Colonial Natives Continuing Ordinance.
16.—Natives Registration Ordinance.
17.—Rhodesia Chamber of Mines Incorporation Ordinance.
18.—Immigration Ordinance.
19.—Town Lands and Outspans Mining Ordinance.
20.—Census Amendment Ordinance.
21.—Appropriation Ordinance.
22.—Municipal Law Further Amendment Ordinance.
23.—Ancient Monuments Protection Ordinance.
24.—Mines and Minerals Amendment Ordinance.

COUNCIL PAPERS, 1901.

Estimates of Expenditure for the Financial Year ending 31st March, 1902.

Agreement entered into for a direct exchange of money orders between the Post Offices of the United Kingdom and Southern Rhodesia.

Convention between the United Kingdom and the United States of America relative to the disposal of real and personal property to which the Administration of this Territory has intimated its intention to adhere.

Agreement entered into between this Administration and the Government of Cape Colony, with reference to the appointment of the Ocean Mail Service.

Report of the Inspector of Schools upon Education for the Year ending 31st March, 1901.

Regulations and Notices promulgated in the *Government Gazette* from the 29th March, 1900 to 27th June, 1901.

Copies of telegrams from His Excellency the High Commissioner, announcing the death of Her Majesty the Queen.

Proclamations relative to the accession of His Majesty King Edward VII., together with a Proclamation by His Majesty requesting all persons in offices of Authority or Government at the time of the decease of Her late Majesty the Queen, to proceed in the execution of their respective offices.

Returns of the informal Census taken on the 31st May, 1901, of the European, Asiatic and Colonial Native Population in Southern Rhodesia.

Report of the Master, Registrar and Sheriff for the Year ended 31st March, 1901.

Report of the Registrar of Deeds, Companies and Patents for the Year ended 31st March, 1901.

Report of the Surveyor General (Department of Lands) for the Year ended 31st March, 1901.

Report of the Medical Director and Principal Medical Officer of the B.S.A. Police for the Year ended 31st March, 1901.

Report of the Acting Postmaster General for the Year ended 31st March, 1901.

Report of the Labour Board of Southern Rhodesia (Salisbury Branch) for the Year ended 31st March, 1901.

Report of the Labour Board of Southern Rhodesia (Bulawayo Branch) for the Year ended 31st March, 1901.

Report of the Chief Native Commissioner (Mashonaland) for the Year ended 31st March, 1901.

Report of the Chief Native Commissioner (Matabeleland) for the Year ended 31st March, 1901.

Report of the Inspector of Native Compounds, Selukwe, for the period from 1st August, 1900 to 31st March, 1901.

Petition from Philip Bourchier Sherard Wrey, styling himself the President, on behalf of the Rhodesia Chamber of Mines, Bulawayo, praying for leave to introduce an Ordinance to provide for the incorporation of the said Chamber.

Statement of Estimated Revenue for the Year ending 31st March, 1902.

Supplementary Estimates of the Expenditure to be defrayed during the Year ending 31st March, 1902.

Part V.

CIVIL ESTABLISHMENT.

These Returns are completed to the 30th September, 1901. An Alphabetical Index to the names of all Civil Servants mentioned in this Return will be found at the commencement of the Volume.

ABBREVIATIONS.

C.	Civil Fees.	O.	Overtime.
C.C. and M.	Civil Commissioner and Magistrate.	P.	On probation (in column for date of fixed appointment).
D.S.	Distributor of Stamps.		
E.	Excise Collector.	P.C.	Periodical Court or Courts.
F.	Forage.	Q	Quarters.
H.	House (Allowance).	R.	Rations.
I.	Interpreting.	T.	Travelling.
L.	Local.	V. M.	Visiting Magistrate.

DIVISION OF HIS HONOUR THE ADMINISTRATOR.

| Office. | Name. | Dates of Appointment. | | | Salary. | Allowance |
		First.	Fixed.	Present.		
					p.a.	
Administrator of Mashonaland and Senior Administrator Southern Rhodesia - -	His Honour W. H. Milton, C.M.G. †	-April 4, '78	April 4, '78	Dec 5, '98	3000	H & 500 entertainment 100
Secretary -	-A. H. Holland †	-Feb 11, '92	Aug 11, '92	Jan 18, '00	500	
Clerk -	-R. A. Blanckenberg	-Mar 1, '95	Mar 1, '95	Dec 8, '98	500	
Legislative and Executive Council.						
Clerk of the Councils -	-Jas. Robertson	-Dec 4, '95	Dec 4, '95	May 1, '99	600	
Caretaker -	-W. N. Colquhoun	-July 1, '01	—	July 1, '01	180	

DIVISION OF CHIEF SECRETARY.

Office.	Name.	First.			Fixed.			Present.			Salary.
Chief Secretary -	-H. H. Castens	-May	1,	'97	May	1,	'97	May	20,	'99	1500
Under Secretary -	-A. B. Rankine	-Sep	5,	'93	Jan	1,	'94	Aug	15,	'01	660
	W. R. Fielde	-May,		'94	May,		'94	Mar	1,	'00	450
	F. Wilson Fox ‡	-May,		'06	Sep	1,	'96	Sep	1,	'96	360
	E. Hope Carson ‡	-Mar	26,	'96	Feb	1,	'97	Feb	1,	'97	360
Clerks -	C. E. Duff * -	-Nov	1,	'94	Nov	4,	'94	Sep	9,	'98	360
	D. McDonald	-Feb	21,	'99	Feb	21,	'00	Feb	21,	'99	360
	J. G. Jearey -	-Nov	29,	'97	Nov	29,	'99	Nov	29,	'97	330
	A. H. Brown	-July	22,	'01	—			July	22,	'01	300
	C. Blackwell	-April	17,	'01	P			April	17,	'01	240
Junior Assistant	-G. Hinds -	-Oct	17,	'98	—			Oct	17,	'98	120

* In Cape Town Office.   † Transferred from Cape Service.   ‡ On Active Service.

Office.	Name.	First.	Fixed.	Present.	Salary.	Allowance.
Accounting Branch.						p. a.
Accountant and Principal Dist. of Stamps	P. E. Craven	Nov 28, '90	Nov 28, '90	April 1, '97	660	
Clerk	H. C. Varley	Sept 1, '95	—	May 23, '98	330	
3 Messengers	at £45, £42, £36 p. a.					
Education.						
Superintending Inspector of Schools and Statist	G. Duthie	June 29, '01	—	June 29, '01	600	†100 & T
Clerk	J. S. Blackwell	Jan 1, '00	April 1, '01	April 1, '00	280	
Capetown Office.						
Government Agent	J. A. Stevens	Dec 4, '90	—	Jan 1, '99	575	*425
Accountant	W. Olive	June 20, '98	June 20, '98	June 20, '98	225	‡325
Clerks	H. T. Goldschmidt	May 5, '91	May, '91	June 1, '99	420	
	A. W. Beadle	April 1, '99	—	April 1, '99	120	‖130
	W. P. Sprigg	Jan 24, '98	—	Jan 24, '98	216	‖ 90
	C. C. Thomas	April 13, '96	June 9, '96	June 9, '96	200	
	R. H. C. Vance	Jan 17, '99	P	Jan 17, '99	180	
	L. Muller	Feb 1, '99	P	Feb 1, '99	100	
Messenger	E. A. Buxton	June, '01	—	June, '91	120	
Chief Accountant.						
Chief Accountant	Thos. Berry	May 26, '90	May 20, '90	July 21, '96	1250	Q
Asst. to do.	R. A. Harbord	April 9, '95	April 1, '98	Oct 1, '98	675	
Bookkeeper	S. F. Morris	Aug 20, '96	Aug 20, '96	Mar 1, '98	400	
Clerks	W. A. Krige	Nov 15, '95	Nov. 15, '95	Dec 21, '96	390	
	G. Short	Mar 7, '98	Mar 7, '98	Mar 7, '98	385	
	E. de L. Scully	Mar 18, '01	P	Mar 18, '01	360	
	A. B. Bell	Aug 4, '99	Aug 1, '01	Aug 4, '99	320	
	A. G. Williams	Nov 1, '94	Dec 5, '00	Mar 15, '98	295	
Messenger					36	
Customs.						
Collector of Customs	E. C. Baxter	July 1, '99	July 1, '00	July 1, '99	1000	
Secretary and Accountant	H. A. Cloete	April, '91	July, '91	July 21, '01	500	O £20
Statistical Clerk	R. A. Myburgh	April 20, '01	P	April 20, '01	240	O 3
Clerk	W. R. Benzies	May 1, '01	P	May 1, '01	240	O 8
Native Messenger	1 at £36 p. a.					
Bulawayo.						
Sub-Collector and Ware house-keeper	A. Bell	Aug 1, '96	Aug 1, '99	Aug 1, '99	600	
Chief Examining Officer	A. E. Speight §	Oct 10, '95	Aug 5, '97	April 16, '01	430	O 73
2nd Examining Officer	G. E. Moss	Sep 6, '00	Sep 6, '01	Oct 1, '01	300	O 10
Clerk and Assistant Ware house-keeper	E. A. Crake	July 1, '99	July 1, '00	April 16, '01	330	O 31
Clerk	G. F. Stapleton	Dec 6, '00	P	Dec 6, '00	270	O 54
1st Class Out-door Officer	C. H. Barrett	April 12, '01	—	April 16, '01	240	—
do.	F. Standing	April 16, '01	—	April 16, '01	240	O 18
do.	J. R. B. Baxter	April 16, '01	—	April 16, '01	240	O 10
2nd Class Out-door Officer	A. Martin	April 16, '01	—	April 16, '01	200	O 1
do.	J. Sybray	May 1, '01	—	May 1, '01	200	O 2
do.	A. W. Byas	Sep 17, '01	—	Oct 1, '01	200	
Native Messengers	2 at £24 p. a.					
Store boys	5 at £36 p. a.					
Salisbury.						
Sub-Collector and Examining Officer	L. L. Bayne §	Feb 1, '93	Dec 24, '93	April 1, '01	500	O 194
Clerk and Warehouse keeper	S. M. Symons	Sep 20, '96	Oct 10, '98	Sep 1, '99	360	
Acting do.	L. G. Jones	July 18, '01	P	July 18, '01	300	O 26

† Statist.　　* Secretary to Rhodesia Railways.　　‡ Accountant to Rhodesia Railways.

‖ Paid by Bechuanaland Railway Company.　　§ Transferred from Cape Service.

Office.	Name.	Dates of Appointment.			Salary.	Allowance.
		First.	Fixed.	Present.		
					p. a.	
1st Class Out-door Officer	R. N. Evans -	Aug 6, '01	—	Aug 6, '01	240	O 36
Locker -	F. R. Snelling	Aug 1, '01	—	Aug 1, '01	180	O 10
Messengers and Store Boys -	2 Natives at £36 p. a.					
Umtali.						
Officer-in-Charge	F. Fisher -	Aug 10, '92	July 9, '00	Aug 1, '01	450	H60 O 68
Out-door Officer	Duties performed by 2 N.C.O.'s of the B. S. A. Police at 2s. 6d. p.d. extra pay.				2/6 p.d.	O 45
Locker -					2/6 p.d.	O 61
Native Messenger	1 at £36 p. a.					
Native Store Boys	6 at £18 p. a.					
Plumtree.						
Officer-in-Charge	T. J. Wadeson	Sep 1, '00	Sep 1, '01	Oct 1, '01	270	L30 O33
Native Messenger	1 at £36 p. a.					
Tuli.						
Customs Officer	Civil Commissioner (Acting)					
Gwanda (Closed).						
Post Office.						
Postmaster General	G. H. Eyre *	Jan 21, '76	Feb 1, '86	Feb 6, '96	1500	H
Secretary -	A. F. Emerton	Feb 6, '97	Feb 6, '97	Sep 1, '97	650	
Accountant -	D. Gillespie -	Feb 17, '97	Feb 17, '97	Sep 1, '97	500	
Chief Clerk -	A. E. Holloway	April 1, '93	April 1, '93	July 31, '97	500	
Secretarial Branch.						
	F. R. Barnes	March 17, '97	Mar 17, '97	May 1, '98	350	
	J. W. Coleman	Dec 10, '96	Dec 10, '96	July 8, '98	300	120 H
Clerks - -	W. A. Devine	Oct 1, '97	Oct 1, '98	Nov 30, '98	275	36 Q
	G. S. S. Gilliland	April 21, '98	April 21, '99	June 13, '00	275	36 Q
	T. H. M. Tobilcock	April 28, '00	April 28, '01	Dec 1, '00	225	120 H
Typist -	Miss A. H. Hunt	April 1, '01	—	April 1, '01	120	
Telegraph Audit Branch.						
Principal Clerk -	J. G. Hunt -	Oct 2, '96	Oct 2, '96	Oct 9, '00	300	48 Q
	J. W. Hewat	Sept 3, '97	Sep 3, '98	Sep 3, '98	275	120 H
Clerks - -	A. W. B. Prew	Nov 17, '98	Nov 17, '99	April 25, '99	250	36 Q
	A. E. Rose -	Aug 16, '99	Dec 23, '00	Aug 16, '99	250	36 Q
Salisbury.						
Postmaster -	T. U. Lapham	Dec 8, '94	Dec 8, '94	Feb 1, '99	350	60 Q
Chief Telegraphist	E. G. Ade -	Nov 14, '96	Nov 14, '96	July 1, '00	300	120 H
Acting Chief Telegraphist	C. H. Westley	Jan 22, '99	Jan 22, '00	Aug 26, '01	250	60 Q
	H. F. Theron	June 28, '98	June 28, '99	Sep 8, '00	275	86 Q
	R. Ellis -	Sep 15, '98	Sep 15, '99	Aug 6, '00	275	36 Q
	P. J. Kennedy	March 1, '01	P	Sep 1, '01	225	36 Q
Assistants -	D. Nunan -	April 11, '00	April 11. '01	April 11, '00	225	36 Q
	H. S. Walker	Jan 5, '01	P	Jan 5, '01	200	36 Q
	W. Smith -	Jan 5, '01	P	Jan 5, '01	200	36 Q
	A. T. Hubbard	March 6, '01	P	April 15, '01	200	Q
	H. Wilmont	July 2, '01	P	July 2, '01	180	36 Q
Learner -	R. Krienke -	May 3, '97	—	May 3, '97	120	
Telephone Switch Clerk	Miss A Marshall	Feb 1, '01	—	Feb 1, '01	150	
Sub-Inspector -	A. Thian -	Sep 18, '95	P	Sep 1, '00	300	36 Q
Mechanician -	J. Thebault -	May 31, '01	P	May 31, '01	200	36 Q
	K. A. Leahy	Dec 16, '95	P	July 1, '00	300	36 Q
Linemen -	L. Newman -	April 1, '01	P	April 1, '01	220	36 Q
	F. G. Sheehan	June 3, '01	P	June 3, '01	200	36 Q
Kopje (Salisbury).						
Postmaster -	P. J. De Stadler	Oct 21, '95	Oct 21, '95	April 30, '98	325	60 Q
Assistant -	A. Russell -	Mar 14, '00	P	Mar 14, '00	225	Q
Bulawayo.						
Surveyor and District Engineer	D. Judson -	Oct 18, '93	Oct 18, '93	Nov 1, '97	500	H
Postmaster -	J. P. A. Powell	March 6, '96	March 6, '96	Aug 1, '97	375	150 H
Chief Postal Assistant	E. C. Harley	Nov 21, '96	Nov 21, '96	Oct 1, '00	300	120 H
Assistants -	J. Read -	Oct 1, '96	Oct 1, '96	June 2, '00	300	120 Q
	N. Barrie -	July 15, '96	July 15, '96	Sep 1, '98	300	36 H 90

* Transferred from Cape Civil Service.

Office.	Name.	First.			Fixed.			Present.			Salary.	Allowance.
											p. a.	
Assistants (*continued*)	A. C. Hunt .	Mar	25,	'98	Mar	25,	'99	Mar	25,	'98	275	36 Q
	D. C. Freeman	April	11,	'00	Apr	11,	'01	Sep	1,	'01	225	36 Q
	E. B. O. Mee	Oct	1,	'99	Oct	1,	'00	Oct	1,	'99	225	36 Q
	W. P. T. Handcock	April	11,	'00	April	11,	'00	April	11,	'00	225	90 H
	V. Redmond	Jan	8,	'00	Jan	8,	'01	Jan	8,	'00	225	36 Q
	J. McGibbony	May	22,	'00	May	22,	'01	May	22.	'00	225	36 Q
	A. Sinclair -	April	11,	'00	April	11,	'01	Nov	26,	'00	225	36 Q
	W. Mann -	Sep	1,	'01		P		Sep	1,	'01	180	36 Q
	F. W. Dennison	June	25,	'01		P		June	25,	'01	180	Q
Supt. Telegraph Office	G. Roberts -	Feb	21,	'96	Feb	21,	'96	Nov	1,	'99	325	60 Q
Actg -Supt. Tel. Office	J. Collyer -	Feb	10,	'97	Feb	10,	'97	Aug	12,	'01	300	60 Q
Telegraphists -	W. Jennings-	April	5,	'96	April	5,	'96	Sep	1,	'01	300	90 H
	P. G. Hunt -	May	6,	'97	May	6,	'98	Feb	12,	'98	300	36 Q
	J. A. Brooks	Aug	11,	'98	Aug	11,	'99	July	7,	'00	275	36 Q
	J. H. Nevitt	Oct	1,	'98	Oct	1,	'99	Oct	1,	'98	250	90 H
	H. R. Evered	April	21,	'99	April	21,	'99	April	21,	'99	250	36 Q
	T. Crago -	Sep	1,	'99	Sep	1,	'00	Sep	1,	'99	250	36 Q
	J. Dobson -	Mar	21,	'00	Mar	21,	'01	May	25,	'00	225	90 H
	T. G. Glanville	Jan	17,	'99	Jan	17,	'99	Jan	17,	'99	250	90 H
	W. H. Trott -	Aug	11,	'00		P		Aug	11,	'00	200	36 Q
	W. J. Dally -	July	21,	'99		P		April	1,	'01	180	36 Q
	F. Rust -	June	8,	'01		P		June	8,	'01	180	36 Q
	R. A. Henman	Mar	7,	'01		P		Mar	7,	'01	200	36 Q
Learners -	J. T. O'Connor	Aug	24,	'99		—		Aug	24,	'99	120	36 Q
	C. Levitt -	Sep	1,	'01		—		Sep	1,	'01	60	
Telephone Switch Clerk	Miss J. M. Kleinschmidt	July	1,	'99		—		July	1,	'99	150	
S. and D. E.'s Clerk	Miss H. G. Elworthy	Aug	1,	'00		—		Aug	1,	'00	150	
Postmaster's Clerk	Miss A. E. Harvey	Aug	21,	'99		—		Aug	21,	'99	150	86 Q
Mechanician -	E. Truan -	Dec	8,	'98		P		Dec	8,	'98	275	36 Q
Linemen -	A. Sellars -	Dec	28,	'97		P		Dec	28,	'97	240	90 Q
	C. Hett -	April	1,	'01		P		April	1,	'01	240	Q
	A. H. Townsend	Oct	30,	'00		P		Oct	30,	'00	200	36 Q
Enkeldoorn.												
Postmr. and Telegraphist	W. H. Macey	Oct	16,	'96	Oct	16,	'96	Mar	15,	'01	300	Q
Lineman -	A. T. Cresswell	Feb	22,	'95		P		April	1,	'01	300	Q
Gwanda.												
Postmr. and Telegraphist	H. R. H. Keen	April	6,	'00		P		Sep	1,	'01	200	36 Q
Gwelo.												
Postmaster -	F. G. Medcalf	May	1,	'96	May	1,	'96	July	17,	'00	300	120 H
Assistants -	O. J. Newton	April	11,	'00		P		Feb	1,	'01	225	Q
	H. E. Earl -	April	14,	'00	April	14,	'01	Sep	12,	'01	225	Q
	R. J. Wakeford	May	31,	'01		P		May	31,	'01	200	Q
Hartley.												
Postmr. and Telegraphist	A. E. Tyler -	Aug	5,	'98	Aug	5,	'99	June	3,	'99	250	Q
Macloutsie.												
Postmr., Telegraphist and Maintenance Officer	H. J. Osborne	Mar	1,	'91	July	1,	'00	Aug	1,	'99	300	36 Q
Palapye.												
Postmr. and Telegraphist	T. H. Harris-	Sep	1,	'99	Sep	1,	'00	Feb	1,	'00	225	Q
Melsetter.												
Postmr. and Telegraphist	H. E. Balch -	June	23,	'98	June	23,	'99	June	1,	'01	250	36 Q
Palapye Station.												
Postmr. and Telegraphist	J. R. Power -	May	4,	'99	July	1,	'00	June	1,	'01	225	Q
Lineman -	A. J. Lambert	Aug	1,	'95		P		July	1,	'98	300	H
Panhalanga.												
Postmr. and Telegraphist	O. W. Webber	May	12,	'96	May	12,	'96	Nov	2,	'97	300	Q
Sebakwe.												
Postmr. and Telegraphist	D. M. O'Leary	May	22,	'00	May	22,	'00	Jan	1,	'01	225	Q
Selukwe.												
Postmr. and Telegraphist	J. Boardman	Oct	1,	'97	Oct	1,	'98	Sep	1,	'00	275	Q
Lineman and Telephonist	G. J. Wetherall	Dec	5,	'00		P		Dec	5,	'00	200	Q

Office.	Name.	First.	Fixed.	Present.	Salary.	Allowance.
Umtali.					p. a.	
Postmaster -	G. H. Wolhuter	Oct 25, '95	Oct 25, '95	Oct 1, '00	300	120 H
Assistants {	C. Eickhoff -	Dec 26, '97	Dec 26, '98	Jan 1, '98	275	36 Q
	L. H. Madgen -	Mar 21, '00	P	Mar 29, '01	200	36 Q
	A. W. Downing	April 11, '00	April 11, '00	April 11, '00	225	36 Q
	D. Bill -	June 25, '01	P	June 25, '01	180	36 Q
Telephone Switch Clerk -	Miss E M.S. Campbell	April 5, '99	—	April 5, '99	150	
Victoria.						
Postmaster and Telegraphist -	H. B. Dooner	Aug 25, '00	P	April 12, '01	200	36 Q
Linemen {	J. MacGregor	Aug 27, '95	P	Aug 27, '95	300	Q
	J. Dunford -	Oct 15, '99	P	April 1, '01	220	Q
Stores Department, Salisbury.						
Clerk in Charge -	E. D. Smith -	June 1, '96	June 1, '96	July 1, '01	480	
Supply Clerk -	C. H. Phelps -	April 1, '98	—	April 1, '98	330	
Accounting Clerk	P. E. Dutton	Nov 17, '98	—	Nov 17, '98	300	
Commissariat Storekeeper	W. Lawson -	Oct 1, '96	—	Jan 1, '97	400	
Commissariat Issuer -	E. Wilson -	April 1, '96	—	June 20, '96	300	
O. C. Transport -	H. C. Lister .	June 20, '96		Feb 1, '97	20/- (p.d.)	{ 46 R, 48 Q, F
Natives, Commissariat Store -	4 @ £24 p.a. R					
Native Messenger -	1 @ £36 p.a.					£10 p.m. while in charge of Stores Dept.
Stores Department, Bulawayo.						
Clerk in Charge -	W. Elliott -	Jan 1, '97	—	July 1, '01	360	
Receiving and Forwarding Clerk -	B. H. Byers	July 15, '96	July 15, '96	Aug 1, '99	400	
Accountant -	O. Cartwright -	April 16, '99	—	April 16, '01	300	£5 p.m. while Accountant to Stores Dept.
Grain and Commissariat Storekeeper	W. J. Slowey	Oct 15, '97	—	Oct 15, '97	300	
Ordinance Store Keeper -	T. R. Clarke	Dec 1, '96	—	May 1, '01	285	
Accountant's Clerk and General Stores Book-Keeper -	E. W. Millar	May 1, '01	—	May 1, '01	240	
Register Clerk -	J. Anderson	May 1, '99	—	May 1, '99	240	
Check Clerk .	N. S. Jones -	Aug 1, '00	—	Jan 20, '01	240	
Health.						
Medical Director and Inspector -	A. M. Fleming	Oct 13, '94	—	April 20, '97	1500	150 H F
Clerk -	J. F. H. Iles -	Nov 1, '00	—	Nov 1, '00	300	
Secretary, Salisbury Hospital -	R. de Vere Cornwell -	April 1, '97	—	April 1, '97	300	60 H
Umtali.						
Hospital Surgeon -	J. Harpur -	Jan 26, '01	—	Jan 26, '01	350	Q
Secretary -	H. B. Watkins -	Mar 19, '97	—	Mar 19, '97	260	Q & R
Gwelo.						
Hospital Surgeon -	H. K. Smyth	Sep 1, '96	—	Sep 1, '96	*200	120 H
Secretary -	R. Macintosh -	Feb 19, '00	—	Feb 19, '00	200	Q & R
Victoria.						
Hospital Surgeon -	M. J. Williams	July 19, '96	—	July 19, '96	*200	
Secretary -	D. T. Phillips -	May 28, '97	—	May 28, '97	200	Q & R
Hartley.						
Hospital Surgeon -	W. M. Eaton -	Feb 10, '99	—	April 1, '00	*100	
Secretary -	J. Scott Gardner -	Mar 12, '00	—	April 1, '01	250	Q & R

* Is also District Surgeon.

Office.	Name.	First.	Fixed.	Present.	Salary.	Allowance.
Gwanda. Hospital Secretary	A. Young	Sep 11, '01	—	Sep 11, '01	200 p. a.	Q & R
Enkeldoorn. Hospital Surgeon	A. D. Owen	Jan 7, '99		April 1, '99	*100	
Native Department Mashonaland.						2 horses, Forage equipment, Cape cart 6 mules.
ChiefNativeCommissioner	H. M. Taberer	June 1, '95	June 1, '95	Nov 1, '95	900	
Asst. do.	W. S. Taberer†	July 7, '91	Jan 1, '94	July 5, '98	550	
Clerks {	D. W. Hook	May 11, '97	May 11, '97	June 2, '00	420	
	A. T. Holland	Jan 11, '98	Jan 11, '99	Jan 6, '01	300	
	R. H. Wood	Aug 15, '00	P	Aug 15, '00	240	
	E. J. Eardley-Mare	July 20, '01	P	July 20, '01	240	
Registrar of Natives	L. F. Bibra §	May 28, '01	—	May 28, '01	2/6	p.d.
Salisbury. Acting Nat. Commissioner	Capt. R. C. Nesbitt, V.C. §	June 15, '01	—	June 15, '01	10/-	p.d.
Charter. Native Commissioner	W. M. Taylor	June 1, '95	—	October, '95	500	2 horses F
Enkeldoorn. Registrar of Natives	G. H. Pidcock	Sep 1, '98	—	Sep 1, '98	60	
Hartley. Native Commissioner	W. E. E. Scott	May, '93	—	April 1, '97	500	2 horses F
Lomagondi. Acting Nat. Commissioner	Lt. C. H. Howell §	Jan 1, '01	—	Jan 1, '01	10/- p.d.	2 horses F
Mazoe (North). Native Commissioner	E. T. Kenny	March, '95	--	July, '98	450	2 horses F
Mazoe (South). Asst. Nat. Commissioner	M. D. Fynn	Oct 6, '99	—	Oct 6, '99	360	2 horses F
M'toko. Acting Nat. Commissioner	F. R. Byron	Nov 1, '97	—	Nov 1, '97	480	2 horses F
M'rewa. Native Commissioner	W. Edwards	May 1, '95		Sep 1, '97	500	2 horses F
Marandella. Native Commissioner	E. W. Morris	March, '93	—	Oct 1, '96	500	2 horses F
Acting do.	H. C. K. Fynn	April 18, '93	Oct 1, '99	April 3, '01	360	£7 10s. p. month while acting.
Makoni. Native Commissioner	A. R. Ross	April 20, '95	—	April 20, '95	500	2 horses F
Um'ali. Native Commissioner and Assistant Magistrate	T. B. Hulley	April 1, '95	—	June 19, '96	550	2 horses F
Clerk	T. A. Raikes	April 1, '00	P	Aug 22, '00	360	
Registrar of Natives	W. S. Wragg	June 1, '93	—	Sep 1, '99	250	
Inyanga. Native Commissioner	—	—	—	—		
Melsetter. Native Commissioner	L. C. Meredith	Nov 1, '94	—	Nov 1, '95	500	2 horses F
Victoria. Native Commissioner	A. Drew	Oct 1, '92	—	Sep 1, '94	500	2 horses F

* Is also District Surgeon.   † Transferred from Cape Service.   § Is also in B.S.A.P.

Office.	Name.	First.		Fixed.		Present.		Salary.	Allowance
Gutu. Native Commissioner	J. H. Williams	Mar 1, '97		—		Mar 1, '97		p. a. 360	2 horsesF
N'danga. Native Commissioner	D. H. Moodie	Nov 1, '96		—		Nov. 15, '00		500	2 horsesF
Chibi. Native Commissioner	P. Forrestall	Oct 1, '94		—		Dec 1, '96		500	2 horsesF
Chilimanzi. Clerk in Charge	J. T. Fisher	Nov 22, '98		—		Dec 18, '99		240	£7 10s p. month whilst acting
Native Department Matabeleland.									2 horses forage, equipment, cart and
Chief NativeCommissioner	H. J. Taylor	Oct 1, '94	Oct 1, '94		May 1, '95		900	6 mules
ChiefClerkandAccountant	F. J. Clarke	July 1, '97		—		July 1, '97		420	
Clerks {	F. C. Campbell	June 1, '08		—		June 1, '08		300	
	E. J. S. Aston	Nov 1, '08		—		Nov 1, '08		300	
	A. Dale	Dec 1, '00		—		Dec 1, '00		270	
	J. C. Makunga	Jan 23, '94	April 1, '01		Jan 23, '94		260	
Relieving Officer	C. G. Fynn	Oct 19, '95		—		April 1, '01		500	
Bubi District. Native Commissioner	R. Lanning	Sep 1, '95		—		Sep 1, '95		500	2 horses, F T Q
Asst. do.	M. W. Barnard	June 1, '09	June 1, '99		June 1, '99		360	1 horse F T Q
Clerk	H. G. Fuller	July 19, '99		—		July 19, '99		270	Q T
Bulilima-Mangwe. Native Commissioner	W. E. Thomas	March 1, '95	Mar 1, '95		Mar 1, '95		500	2 horses, F & T, Draws 60 personal and 72 Q allowances
Asst. do.	T. M. Thomas	Mar 1, '97		—		March 1, '97		360	1 horse, F T Q
Clerk	E. D. Taylor	Dec 1, '98		—		Dec 1, '98		300	Q & T
Matobo District. Native Commissioner	H. M. G. Jackson	Oct 14, '95		—		Oct 14, '95		500	2 horses, F T Q
Asst. do	H. A. Elliott	July 27, '99		—		July 27, '99		360	1 horse, F T Q
Clerk	H. F. Greer	July 1, '99		—		July 1, '99		300	Q & T
A. N. C.	P. A. Stuart	Sep 7, '97		—		Sep 7, '97		360	1 horse, Q & T
Insiza District. Native Commissioner	A. A. Campbell	Nov 1, '96		—		Nov 1, '96		500	2 horses, F T Q
Asst. do.	L. G. Robinson	Feb 1, '97		—		July 1, '97		400	1 horse, F T Q
Clerk	A. L. Jones	June 12, '99		—		June 12, '99		300	Q & T
Belingwe District. Native Commissioner and Assistant Magistrate	S. N. G. Jackson	Nov 1, '95		--		June 6, '01		500	2 horses, F T Q
Asst. Nat. Commissioner	J. W. Posselt	April 15, '97		—		April 15, '97		400	2 horses, F T Q
Clerk	W. A. King	July 1, '99		—		July 1, '99		270	Draws 30 as Clerk to A. M. Q & T
Gwelo and Selukwe Native Commissioner and Assistant Magistrate	C. T. Stuart	Nov 1, '96		—		April 1, '01		550	2 horses, F & T

| Office. | Name. | Dates of Appointment. | | | Salary. | Allowance |
		First.	Fixed.	Present.		
Gwelo—(Con.)					p.a.	
Clerk and Registrar of Natives	- G. D. Dunbar	Nov 1, '99	—	Nov 1, '99	270	Q & T
Clerk	- J. W. Reid	July 26, '01	—	July 26, '01	240	Q & T
Tuli District.						1 horse,
Asst. Nat. Commissioner	J. F. Gordon	Dec 1, '95	—	Sep 1, '96	360	F T Q
Sebungwe-Mafungabusi and Wankie District.						100 local, 2 horses,
Native Commissioner	C. L. Carbutt	Feb 6, '97	—	June 1, '99	500	F T Q
Asst. do.	W. E. Farrer	May 19, '99	—	May 19, '99	360	1 horse, F T Q
Asst. do.	W. F. Gowers	Jan 1, '99	—	May 1, '00	360	1 horse, F T Q
Asst. do.	H. H. de Laessoe	Feb 19, '00	—	April 11, '01	360	1 horse, F T Q .
Fingoe Location.						1 horse,
Superintendent	H. F. Griffith	Mar 25, '97	—	Oct 1, '98	500	F T Q
Division No. 1—						2 horses,
Inspr. N. Compounds	F. G. Elliott	Nov 1, '97	—	Aug 1, '00	500	6 mules, F T Q
Division No. 2—						1 horse,
Inspr. N. Compounds	W. A. Tilney	April 15, '97	—	July 1, '01	400	6 mules, F T Q
Division No. 3—						1 horse,
Inspr. N. Compounds	C. B. Cooke	Dec 1, '95	—	July 1, '01	500	6 mules, F T & 60 Q allowance
Stationery and Printing Department.						
Superintendent	H. Cordner	Aug 1, '94	Aug 1, '94	Mar 1, '99	480	
Clerk	W. Low	Aug 4, '00	P	Aug 4, '00	300	
Auditor.						
Auditor and Inspector	P. D. L. Fynn §	Nov 15, '89	Feb 24, '94	April 1, '99	800	
Chief Examiner	A. G. Pett §	Feb 13, '91	Nov 6, '92	April 1, '99	500	
Examiner of Revenue	C. Short	May 13, '95	May 13, '95	April 1, '97	480	
Examiners of Expenditure Accounts	E. H. Smith-Wright	July 19, '95	July 19, '95	Oct 1, '97	420	† 50
	C. H. C. Boardman	Oct 12, '92	Oct 12, '92	Mar 1, '98	420	
	W. T. Laing §	Feb 18, '95	Oct 8, '05	May 2, '99	390	
	S. T. Dunbar	May 18, '96	May 18, '96	Mar 1, '99	390	
Temporary Clerk	A. H. Newnham	April 26, '95	—	April 1, '01	270	
Clerk	W. H Orpen	Dec 13, '99	P	Dec 13, '99	200	
Messenger	1 at £42 p.a.					
Bulawayo.						
Accountant	S. V. Cloete	April 1, '98	April 1, '93	May 1, '98	660	* 140
Clerks	N. H. Chataway	Mar 27, '96	Mar 27, '96	May 1, '98	450	† 50
	W. M. Donald	Mar 19, '00	P	Mar 19, '00	240	
Messenger	1 at £30 p.a.					

DIVISION OF ATTORNEY-GENERAL.

Office.	Name.	First.	Fixed.	Present.	Salary.	Allowance
Attorney-General	J. G. Kotze	Aug 1, '00	Aug 1, '00	Aug 1, '00	1500	H 250
Draughtsman and Additional Law Officer	Ad-Sir T. C. Scanlen, K.C.M.G.	Oct, '94	—	Oct, '94	2000	
Secretary to Law Dept.	C. Bayley	Nov 1, '90	Nov 1, '93	March 1, '95	600	
Acting do.	R. McIlwaine §	Dec 2, '95	Dec 2, '96	April 19, '01	600	
Clerk	W. D. Stewart	Sep 15, '98	Aug 1, '01	Aug 1, '00	330	

§ Transferred from Cape Service.　　　† Secretary to Tender Board.　　　* Paid out of Special Account.

Office.	Name.	Dates of Appointment.			Salary.	Allowance.
		First.	Fixed.	Present.		
Bulawayo.						p. a.
Solicitor General	C. H. Tredgold	July 1, '98	Sep 1, '00	Sep 1, '00	1200	
Clerks	A. C. Kirby	Feb 26, '95	Oct 1, '97	Jan 1, '00	600	
	K. D. Peacock	Feb 22, '00	P	Aug 1, '01	180	
High Court of Southern Rhodesia.						
Salisbury.						
Judge	Hon. J. P. F. Watermeyer	July, '96	July, '96	July, '96	1750	250 H
Master and Registrar	J. H. Kennedy*	Sep 1, '91	Sep 1, '91	Nov 1, '94	1000	
Acting Chief Clerk	W. T. Biddulph	Mar, '96	Aug 1, '96	July 1, '99	400	
Clerk	A. W. Redfern	April 6, '98	Jan 18, '01	July 17, '99	330	
Additional Asst. Registrar	K. B. Fairbairn†	Jan 1, '99	Jan 1, '99	Jan 1, '99	330	
Clerk	H. McIlwaine	Dec 28, '98	Dec 28, '99	July 12, '01	300	
Bulawayo.						
Judge	Hon. J. Vintcent	July 1, '94	Sep 10, '94	Dec 20, '98	2000	H & T
Assistant Registrar	C. F. Granger	Aug 17, '96	Aug 17, '96	July 6, '99	500	
Judge's Clerk	S. P. Mellor	Jan 1, '98	—	Mar 15, '98	330	
Clerk	G. M. Kirschbaum	June 6, '01	—	June 6, '01	240	
Registrar of Deeds and Companies.						
Salisbury.						
Registrar	G. J. King	Feb 1, '95	Feb 1, '95	April 1, '97	600	
Clerk	W. W. Tucker	Aug 20, '96	Aug 20, '96	July 1, '97	400	
Bulawayo.						
Registrar	A. R. onge	Sep 1, '96	Sep 1, '96	May 16, '00	500	
Clerk	E. B. S. Mercer	Oct 25, '99	—	July 23, '00	300	
District Courts and Offices.						
Salisbury.						
Civil Commissioner	G. W. Farmaner	Sep 15, '91	Sep 15, '91	Dec 1, '98	630	
Chief Clerk	(Vacant).					
Clerk	E. C. Sharp	April 1, '94	Feb 1, '97	April 1, '00	400	
Clerk and Distributor of Stamps	P. D. Myburgh	Feb 1, '97	Feb 1, '97	Nov 1, '98	400	
Junior Assistant	A. Bain	Feb 1, '01	—	Feb 1, '01	72	
Messenger	1 at £5 p.m.					
Magistrate	E. A. L. Brailsford	Aug, '30	July, '82	Nov 1, '98	800	H 120, horse F
Acting Assistant Magistrate	G. H. McCulloch	Jan 30, '95	Aug 18, '99	May 1, '01	500	
Clerks	A. M. J. R. Peel	April 1, '98	April 1, '99	April 1, '98	330	
	C. Crewe	June 20, '00	June 20, '01	June 20, '00	300	
Interpreter (*vacant*).						
Bulawayo.						250 H,
Civil Commissioner	H. Marshall Hole	April 25, '90	April 25, '90	July 1, '01	1250	horse & F
Clerk	W. H. Adcock	July 6, '97	Jan 1, '99	July 1, '01	450	
Asst. Civil Commissioner	W. H. L. Honey	Dec 1, '93	Dec 1, '93	July 1, '01	700	7s. 6d. per diem as Acting C. C., horse & F
Clerks	A. Nell	Mar 8, '96	Mar 8, '96	Aug 1, '97	450	
	G. T. J. Harris	July 3, '97	Feb 1, '99	Sep 21, '97	400	
	J. Milton	June 20, '98	April 1, '99	June 20, '98	400	
	R. B. Harper	Feb 13, '99	July 6, '00	July 6, '99	320	
	F. J. M. Smith	Jan 9, '99	Aug 17, '01	July 1, '01	240	
Magistrate	L. Powys Jones §	Dec 1, '79	Mar 8, '81	Feb 26, '97	900	Q horse F
Assistant Magistrates	C. A. Pidcock	Nov 27, '97	Aug 1, '98	Aug 1, '98	540	
	G. le Sueur	Dec 29, '92	Aug 21, '93	Oct 5, '99	480	
	E. J. Lawlor	April 11, '98	Aug 1, '99	Nov 1, '00	420	10s. per diem
	C. M. Fletcher	Aug 19, '96	Aug 19, '96	Aug 19, '96	450	
Clerks	W. R. Blanckenberg	July 14, '99	July 14, '00	July 14, '99	300	
	H. Rangeley	Sep 1, '00	—	Sep 1, '00	300	
Messenger of Court	7s. p.d. & Court Fees.					

---

* Also High Sheriff of Southern Rhodesia.   † Also acts as Clerk to Hon. Mr Justice Watermeyer.
§ Transferred from Cape Civil Service.

Office.	Name.	Dates of Appointment.			Salary.	Allowance.
		First.	Fixed.	Present.		
Umtali.					p. a.	200 Q,
Civil Commissioner and						
Magistrate -	R. H. Myburgh‡	Jan 23, '85	Feb 1, '86	Oct 1, '98	800	2 horses F
Assistant Magistrate	T. B. Hulley §	April 1, '95	Nov 1, '00	Mar 22, '00	—	
Chief Clerk -	A. L. Baker -	May 1, '95	Sep 19, '96	April 2, '00	400	
Clerks	H. P. Miles -	May 2, '96	May 2, '96	May 2, '96	360	
	F. A. Yates -	June 16, '96	June 15, '96	Oct 1, '97	360	
	F. M. Leigh-Lye	Dec 1, '00	—	Dec 1, '00	240	
	P. F. Gilbert	May 22, '01	P	May 22, '01	180	
Interpreter -	R. O'Reilly	Mar 15, '99	.	Mar 15, '99	300	
						P C 100 F
Gwelo.						1 horse,
Civil Commissioner and						& 4 mules
Magistrate -	P. G. Smith	July 11, '94	July 11, '94	July 13, '97	800	Q
Actg. Asst. Magistrate	C. W. Cary -	April 15, '92	Jan 1, '96	Sep 10, '01	420	L, 7/6
Clerk and Distributor of						per diem
Stamps -	H. C. Quin -	Sep 1, '95	Sep 1, '95	Feb 1, '97	360	
C.C. Clerk -	F. R. Thomas	Sep 1, '98	Mar 1, '00	Sep 1, '98	360	
M. Clerk & Interpreter	C. F. W. Nauhaus	April 1, '01	—	April 1, '01	360	
Victoria.						Q & F,
Civil Commisssioner and						Fees £1 1/
Magistrate -	G. M. Huntley	Feb 20, '98	Aug 1, '00	Nov 14, '98	600	
Clerks -	H. W. Hearn	April 27, '97	P	Nov 21, '97	330	
	C. J. R. Gardiner	Jan 1, '00	P	Jan 1, '00	300	
						£120 in
Melsetter.						lieu of
Civil Commissioner and						horses,
Magistrate -	W. M. Longden	June 1, '91	June 1, '91	Oct 7, '95	600	etc.
Clerks -	E. Hoal -	Nov 16, '94	Nov 16, '94	Jan 1, '96	360	
	L. F. H. Roberts	June, '98	July 1, '99	Jan 1, '99	300	
						H 80 F,
Manzingama.						2 horses
Civil Commissioner and						& 2 mules
Magistrate -	J. P. L. de Smidt‡	Jan 2, '90	July 2, '90	Jan 6, '99	500	Q
Clerk and D. S. -	T. J. Coltsman Cronin	Mar 8, '00	P	Mar 8, '00	270	
Clerk and Interpreter	S. W. Greer -	Oct 8, '00	P	Oct 8, '00	240	
Messenger -	1 at £3 10s. per month					
Enkeldoorn.						
Acting Assistant Magis-						
trate - -	W. R. Shandt‡	April 21, '88	Mar 17, '89	May 15, '01	480	
Clerk -	G. H. Pidcock	April 27, '98	—	April 27, '98	300	Also
						draws 60
						as Regis-
						trar of
						Natives
Prisons.						at Enkel-
						doorn.
Salisbury.						
Gaoler -	P. Hyland -	Jan 1, '97	Jan 1, '97	Jan 1, '97	325	R Q F
Matron -	J. Hyland -	Aug 1, '99	—	Aug 1, '99	30	Q & R
Chief Warder -	W. S. Barbour	May 14, '98	—	April 20, '00	12/-	Q & R
Warders -	2 at 10s. p.d., Q & R, 5 at 8s.	3 at 9s. p.d, Q & R, and p.d., Q & R.			p.d.	
Native Warders -	3 at £4 p.m. Q & R, and 4 at £3 per month, Q & R					
Bulawayo.						
Gaoler -	T. Smith -	June 13, '95	—	June 13, '95	325	Q & R
Matron -	M. Smith -	Oct 14, '97	—	Oct 14, '97	60	Q & R
Warders -	1 at 12s. p.d., 6 at 8s.	p.d., 8 at 7s p.m. and 4 at £3 p.m.	p.d., 1 at £4			
Gwelo.						
Gaoler -	P. Sandilands	Dec 1, '97	—	Oct 15, '98	240	Q & R
Acting Gaoler -	J. Jackson -	Aug 1, '98	—	July 1, '01	10/-	p.d. Q&R
Matron -	J. H. Sandilands	May 1, '00	—	May 1, '00	40	R
Warders -	2 at 7s. p.d., Q & R					
Native Warders	2 at £4 p.m., 1 at £3 p.m., 3 at £2 p.m.					

‡ Transferred from Cape Civil Service. § Also Native Commissioner.

Office.	Name.	Dates of Appointment.			Salary.	Allowance.
		First.	Fixed.	Present.		
Umtali.						p. a.
Gaoler -	J. J. Healy - -	April 23, '98	—	Sep 1, '00	240	Q & R
Turnkey -	1 at 10s. p.d., Q and R	—	—	—		
Warders -	4 at 7s. p.d., Q and R	---	—	—		
Native Warders -	5 at £4 p.m., Q and R	—	—	—		
Victoria.						
Gaoler -	J. Maughan - -	Oct 1, '97	—	May 18, '00	240	Q & R
Turnkey -	1 at £144, Q and R	—	—	—		
Warders -	2 at £36 p.a., 3 at £30 p.a.		—	—		
Manzingama.						
Gaoler -	H. Robinson -	May 20, '00	—	May 20, '00	180	Q & R
Native Warders -	2 at 50s. p.m., Q and R	—	—	—		
Constabulary.						
Mashonaland.						150 H
						horse & F
Chief Inspector -	J. W. Fuller -	Sep 12, '98	—	Sep 12, '98	600	for two
Inspector -	J. de G. Birch	April 3, '96	—	Jan 1, '01	475	48 H,
						horse & F
Sub-Inspector -	D. M. Lewis	April 22, '97	—	Oct 17, '00	365	48 H, 45 R
						horse & F
Sub-Inspector and Licence Inspector -	H. J. K. Brereton	Jan, '97	--	Mar 1, '01	365	48 H, horse & F
1st Class Sergeants	{ 1 at £274, H 48 & R	—	—	—		
	{ 2 at £274 R					
2nd Class Sergeants	4 at 14s p.d., R	—	—	—		
3rd Class Sergeants	3 at 12s. p.d., R	--	—	—		
1st Class Constables	5 at 10s. p.d., R	--	—	—		
2nd Class Constables	7 at 9s. p.d., R	—	—	---		
3rd Class Constables	17 at 8s. p.d., R	—	—	—		
Mounted Constables	4 at 8s. p.d., R	—	--	—		
1st Class Detective	1 at 15s. p.d., R	—	—	—		
2nd Class Detective	1 at 14s. p.d., R	—	—	—		
3rd Class Detective	1 at 12s. p.d., R	—	—	—		
1st Class Native Sergeant	1 at 110s. p m.	--	---	—		27 R
2nd Class Native Sergeant	1 at 90s. p.m.	—	—	—		do
Native Constables	27 at 60s. p.m.	—	—	--		do
Native Interpreter	1 at 100s. p.m.	—	—	---		do
Matabeleland.						
Chief Inspector and Head of Detective and Licence Departments -	F. W. Smith §	June 10, '81	Nov 24, '98	Nov 24, '98	600	Q
Inspector -	F. Rice -	Jan 23, '95	April 25, '98	Jan 1, '01	475	H
	{ D. W. Stewart	Nov 28, '95	Aug 21, '98	Aug 21, '98	420	H
Sub-Inspectors -	{ J. W. Macdougall	Jan 18, '95	Oct 6, '98	Oct 6, '98	400	H
	{ M. Breen -	Jan 12, '97	Feb 9, '01	Feb 9, '01	365	H
Chief Clerk -	H. J. Nanson	Jan 1, '99	Jan 1, '99	Jan 1, '99	365	H
Assistant Clerks	{ A. E. Edge -	Dec 16, '90	—	Aug 18, '00	274	Q
	{ A. M. Dickson	Jan 2, '01	—	Feb 20, '01	220	H
1st Class Sergeants	{ 4 at 16s. p.d.,	—	--	—		
	{ 3 at 15s. p.d., Q	—	--	—		
2nd Class Sergeants	5 at 14s. p.d., Q	—	—	—		
3rd Class Sergeants	3 at 12s. p.d., Q	—	—	—		
1st Class Constables	3 at 12s. p.d., Q	—	—	—		
3rd Class Constables	57 at 10s. p.d.	—	—	—		
Chief Detective	Thomas Kyd	Dec 1, '78	Feb 1, '99	Mar 1, '00	384	H
1st Class Detectives	3 at 15s. p.d.	—	—	—		H
2nd Class Detectives	3 at 14s. p.d.	—	—	—		H
3rd Class Detectives	3 at 12s. p.d.	—	—	—		H
Native Detectives	4 at 3s. 6d. p.d., Q	—	—	—		
Native Sergeants	2 at £7 10s. p.m., Q	—	--	—		
Native Constables	19 at £4 10s. p.m., Q	--	—	—		
Native Driver -	1 at £2 10s., p.m., Q	—	—	—		
Native Servants	2 at 15s. p.m., Q	—	—	—		

§ Transferred from Cape Service.

Office.	Name.	First.	Fixed.	Present.	Salary.	Allowance.
						Draws 1000 as Commr. Public Works Temp'y 25 p m.
Commissioner of Mines	T. Griffin	Oct 10, '94	Oct 10, '94	Oct 1, '97	1000 p.a.	
Registrar of Claims	E. W. S. Montagu	July 16, '98	—	April 1, '99	720	
	N. Macglashan	Sep 1, '90	Sep 1, '90	Oct 5, '97	1000	H 150, horse 60
	G. J. Bowen	Sep 1, '92	Sep 1, '92	Mar 1, '94	750	horse 60
Mining Commissioners	C. D. Fleming	Oct 28, '95	- -	April 1, '99	600	horse 60
	O. H. Ogilvie	June 1, '95	-	April 1, '98	480	horse 60
	A. A. I. Heyman	July 1, '98	-	Aug 1, '00	480	horse 60
Claim Inspectors and	J. A. D. Hawksley	Oct 1, '95	—	April 1, '97	480	
Clerks	F. S. Broun	July 15, '97	—	July 15, '97	480	
	C. M. Campbell	Sep 15, '95	—	April 1, '98	420	
Assistant do.	E. G. Beaty-Pownall	Oct 19, '96	—	April 1, '97	420	
	A. C Bagshawe	Aug 5, '97	—	Aug 5, '97	480	
	G. N. Fleming	June 20, '97	—	Feb 22, '98	480	
	H. P. Selmes	Mar 11, '98	—	Mar 11, '98	480	
	H. U. Spreckley	July 1, '95	- -	July 1, '95	360	
	S. B. Norris	June 1, '94	—	April 1, '95	360	
	C. J. S. Hopgood	Dec 1, '98	—	Dec 1, '98	360	
	B. A. M.M. Helm	Mar 15, '99	- -	Mar 15, '99	360	
	C. E. Slocock	April 1, '99	-	April 1, '99	360	
	G. H. James	June 19, '99	—	June 19, '99	360	
	W. J. Hiscock	July 17, '99	—	July 17, '99	360	
	E. T. Bolling	Aug 24, '99	- -	Aug 24, '99	360	
Clerks	G. L. B. Critchley-Salmonson	Oct 4, '98	- -	Oct 4, '98	300	
	A. J. Grimaldi	Feb 1, '00	—	Feb 1, '00	300	
	J. H. Melville	Aug 9, '00	- -	Aug 9, '00	300	
	P. F. Hone	Aug 29, '00	—	Aug 29, '00	300	
	C. F. H. Monro	Aug 29, '00	- -	Aug 29, '00	300	
	B. F. Bagshawe	Feb 1, '01	—	Feb 1, '01	240	
	J. C E. Douglas	Feb 8, '01	—	Feb 8, '01	240	
	A. G. Helm	July 1, '01	- -	July 1, '01	240	
	E. H. J. Stewart	July 19, '01	—	July 19, '01	240	
	S. G. R. White	July 26, '01	—	July 26, '01	240	
	A. R. Hone	Aug 21, '01	—	Aug 21, '01	240	
Surveyor to Mines Department	C. H. Rivers	July 19, '00	- -	July 19, '00	700	Field 300
Commr. of Public Works	T. Griffin	Oct 10, '94	Oct 10, '94	Oct 1, '97	1000	Draws 1000 as Commr. of Mines
Chief Inspector	H. Ashmead	Jan 6, '00	Jan 6, '00	Jan 6, '00	840	T
Inspector	S. J. Oliphant	May 9, '99	Mar 12, '96	Aug 1, '99	600	60 horse
Do.	H. B. Douslin	June 1, '97	Jan 26, '00	June 1, '97	600	60 horse
Assistant do.	M. Russell	April 1, '97	—	April 1, '97	420	
	J. C. J. Coope	Jan 1, '92	Jan 1, '92	Jan 1, '92	500	550 T, 200 special
Inspectors of Roads	C. W. Briggs	Aug 1, '99	- -	Aug 1, '99	500	425 T and equipment
Paymaster	H. A. Harper	Feb 1, '90	—	June 8, '99	500	
Chief Clerk	C. G. Laurie	June 1, '95	—	June 5, '00	420	
Draughtsman	P. G. R. Harvey	Jan 23, '99	—	July 22, '00	420	
Clerk and Storekeeper	T. W. F. Townsend	June 15, '00	—	June 15, '00	330	
Clerk and Draughtsman	P. C. Farquharson	Aug 12, '99	—	Aug 12, '99	300	
Foreman of Works	T. N. Amos	April 1, '00	—	April 1, '00	420	

Office.	Name.	Dates of Appointment.			Salary.	Allowance.
		First.	Fixed.	Present.		

DIVISION OF SURVEYOR-GENERAL.

Office.	Name.	First.	Fixed.	Present.	Salary.	Allowance.
					p. a.	horse F, cart and mules
Surveyor-General	J. M. Orpen	Jan 5, '97	Jan 5, '97	Jan 5, '97	2000	
Secretary Lands and Agriculture	E. Ross Townsend	June 3, '95	June 3, '95	April 1, '01	1100	F H
Acting Examiner of Diagrams	H. G. E. J. E. Sawerthal	Nov, '92	Nov, '92	Feb 28, '01	800	
Clerks	W. Cole	ay 16, '95	May 16, '95	May 16, '95	450	
	F. H. S. Lee	April 1, '01	—	April 1, '01	300	
	N. L. K. Eddie	Jan 6, '00	P	Nov 1, '00	270	
	C. F. Hinds	Jan 16, '99	—	Jan 16, '99	100	
Junior Assistants	Miss B. de Bruno Austin	July 8, '01	—	July 8, '01	120	
Draughtsman	C. J. Matthews	May 15, '95	Jan 23, '01	May 15, '95	500	
Asst. Draughtsman	A. Stidolph	Jan 16, '99	P	Jan 16, '99	330	
Surveyor and Assistant Examiner	W. J. Atherstone	June 29, '98	P	May 1, '01	560	
Clerk and Assistant to Examiner of Diagrams	A. H. Matthews	Sep 18, '99	P	Sep 18, '99	300	
Agriculture.						
Clerk and Registrar of Brands	M. A. Lingard	May, '92	May, '92	April 1, '97	480	
Clerks	W. C. Hurrell	April 1, '99	—	April 1, '99	360	
	J. D. Tennant	May 9, '01	P	Oct 1, '01	300	
Veterinary Branch.						horse, F Q, £1 p.m.
Chief Vet. Surgeon and Chief Inspr. of Cattle	C. E. Gray, M.R.C.V.S.	Jan 1, '96	—	April 17, '97	500	st'ble boy H F Q
Vet. Surgeon and Cattle Inspr., Umtali	E. M Jarvis, M.R.C.V.S.	Jan 16, '01	—	Jan 16, '01	480	£1 p.m. st'ble boy
Cattle Inspr., Salisbury	H. G. Morris	Feb 1, '01	—	Feb 1, '01	300	H F Q, £1 p.m. st'ble boy
Cattle Inspr., Salisbury District	C. de K. Birch	Feb 1, '99	—	Feb 1, '99	300	H F Q, £1 p.m. st'ble boy
Cattle Inspr., Charter	A. Strickland	Mar 28, '97	—	Mar 28, '97	300	
Do. Enkeldoorn	G. W. Cumming	Mar 12, '98	—	Mar 12, '98	300	H F
Do. Victoria	E. A. Farmery	Feb 1, '97	—	Feb 1, '97	300	H F Q
Do Melsetter	C. E. Orpen	July 1, '00	—	July 1, '00	300	H F
Matabeleland.						H F Q, 2 boys, private practice
Vet. Surgeon, Bulawayo	J. M. Sinclair, M.R.C.V.S.	Mar 2, '99	—	Mar 2, '99	500	
Do. do.	J. J. Gorman, M.R.C.V.S.	Feb 12, '97	—	Feb 12, '97	480	H F
Cattle Inspectors, Bulawayo	J. D. F. Fernside	May 5, '01	—	May 23, '01	300	H F
	F. X. Kearney	Mar 9, '01	—	Mar 9, '01	300	H F
	C. E. P. Weinand	June 12, '01	—	June 12, '01	300	H F
	F. W. Yates	June 17, '01	—	June 17, '01	300	H F
Cattle Inspr., Bembezi	— Cameron	Oct 1, '00	—	Oct 1, '00	300	H F
Do., Mangwe	ans Lee	July 10, '01	—	July 10, '01	10	p.m.
Do., Gwelo	G. Tomlinson, M.R.C.V.S.	June 15, '00	—	June 15, '00	5/	p.d. B.S.A.P.
Do., Gwanda	G. Cooke	Feb 1, '01	—	Feb 1, '01	300	H F
Do., Gwelo	W. C. Dilworth	May 14, '00	—	May 14, '00	300	H F

Office.	Name.	Dates of Appointment.			Salary.	Allowance.
		First.	Fixed.	Present.		

DIVISION OF TERRITORIAL DEFENCE.

Office.	Name.	First.			Fixed.	Present.			Salary.	Allowance.
Headquarter's Staff.										Paid by
Commandant General, Colonel	R. Chester Master	July,		'01	—	July,		'01	p. a.	Imperial Govt.
Chief Staff Officer	(Vacant)	—			—	—				
Chief Paymaster, Major	R. H. Everett	Nov	1,	'96	—	Nov	1,	'96	600	R Q
Principal Medical Officer (also Medical Director)	A. M. Fleming, C.M.G.	April	1,	'97	—	April	1,	'97	600	
Matabeleland.										
Commandant, Lieut.-Col.	W. Bodle	Nov	1,	'96	—	Sep	27,	'98	600 p.d.	R Q
Chief Inspector, Major	M. Straker	Nov	1,	'96	—	Jan	5,	'99	25/	R Q
	F. L. Bowden	Nov	1,	'96	—	Nov	1,	'96	20/	R Q
Inspectors, Captains	J. Carden (seconded, Barotseland Police)	Nov	1,	'96	—	April	13,	'98		
	A. P. L. Cazalet	Nov	1,	'96	—	Jan	5,	'99	20/	R Q
	H. Chawner	Nov	1,	'96	—	Oct	22,	'97	20/	R Q
	G. V. Drury	Nov	1,	'96	—	Nov	1,	'96	20/	R Q
Sub-Inspectors, Lieutenants	R. Cashel (seconded, S.R.V. Western Division)	Nov	1,	'99	—	Sep	1,	'99		
	H. Chapman	Oct	20,	'99	...	Oct	20,	'99	15/6	R Q
Surgeon Lieutenant	E. T. Clayton	Dec	4,	'00	—	Dec	4,	'00	500 p.d.	p.a., R Q
Sub-Inspector, Lieut., Quartermaster	R. H. Griffith	July	1,	'01	—	July	1,	'01	26/	R Q
Sub-Inspectors, Lieutenants	F. A. Hodson	Mar	29,	'01	—	Mar	29,	'01	15/6	R Q
	J. S. Ingham	Mar	22,	'00	—	Mar	22,	'00	15/6	R Q
Sub-Inspector, Lieut., Paymaster	L. C. Masterson	Nov	19,	'00	—	Nov	19,	'00	20/	R Q
	W. E. Murray	Nov	1,	'96	—	Nov	1,	'96	15/6	R Q
	A. B. Phipps	Jan	26,	'98	—	Jan	26,	'98	15/6	R Q
Sub-Inspectors, Lieutenants	S. Spain	Feb	1,	'97	—	Feb	1,	'97	15/6	R Q
	G. Stops	Sep	6,	'00	—	Sep	6,	'00	15/6	R Q
	W. E. St. John	Jan	5,	'99	—	Jan	5,	'99	15/6	R Q
	A. J. Tomlinson	Nov	1,	'96	—	Nov	1,	'96	15/6	R Q
	Hon. W. Yarde-Buller	May	25,	'99	—	May	25,	'99	15/6	R Q
Mashonaland.										
Commandant, Lieut.-Colonel	J. Flint	Nov	22,	'99	—	Nov	22,	'99	600 p.d.	R Q
Chief Inspectors, Majors	A. V. Gosling	Nov	1,	'96	—	Nov	1,	'96	25/	R Q
	H. H. Hopper	Nov	1,	'96	—	Nov	1,	'96	25/	R Q
Inspectors, Captains	C. H. Gilson	Nov	1,	'96	—	Aug	8,	'97	20/	R Q
	W. J. Macqueen	Nov	1,	'96	—	Feb	16,	'97	20/	R Q
Inspector, Captain, Paymaster	C. F. L. Money	Nov	1,	'96	—	Aug	10,	'97	25/	R Q
	C. F. L. Monro	Nov	1,	'96	—	Aug	10,	'97	20/	R Q
Inspectors, Captains	R. C. Nesbitt, V.C.	Nov	1,	'96	—	Nov	1,	'96	20/	R Q
	G. H. P. Williams	Nov	1,	'96	—	April	27,	'01	20/	R Q
	F. H. Addison	Dec	7,	'97	—	Dec	7,	'97	15/6	R Q
	F. E. Eastwood	Feb	16,	'97	—	Feb	16,	'97	15/6	R Q
	K. Greenway	April	3,	'01	—	April	3,	'01	15/6	R Q
Sub-Inspectors, Lieutenants	P. Gwynne	Nov	1,	'96	—	Nov	1,	'96	15/6	R Q
	H. H. C. Hardy	July	13,	'01	...	July	13,	'01	15/6	R Q
	A. M. Harte Barry	Jan	1,	'98	—	Jan	1,	'98	15/6	R Q
	C. H. Howell	April	6,	'00	—	April	6,	'00	15/6	R Q
	R. H. Lidderdale	—			—	—				

CIVIL ESTABLISHMENT.

Office.	Name.	Dates of Appointment.			Salary.	Allowance.
		First.	Fixed.	Present.		
Sub-Inspector, Lieut., Quartermaster	T. S. Masterman	- Oct 29, '98	--	Oct 29, '98	p.d. 26/	R Q
Sub-Inspectors, Lieutenants {	W. H. Moore	- April 19, '98	—	April 19, '98	15/6	R Q
	M. H. G. Mundell	- Dec 1, '98	.	Dec 1, '96	15/6	R Q
	A. de M. Myburgh	- April 3, '01	—	April 3, '01	15/6	R Q
	J. Tait -	- April 6, '00	...	April 6, '00	15/6	R Q
Volunteers.						horse F and equip- ment
Staff Officer -	- Major P. W. Forbes	- Nov 16, '89	Nov 16, '89	Oct 24, '98	p.a. 800	
2 Adjutants -	- £500 p.a., horse, F and equipment		—	—		

Office.	Name.	First.	Fixed.	Present.	Salary.	Allowance

NORTH-EASTERN RHODESIA.

Office.	Name.	First.	Fixed.	Present.	Salary.	Allowance
Head Office.						H & 180
					p. a.	enter-
Administrator -	R. Codrington	June, '98	—	June, '00	800	tainm'nt
Private Secretary	Vacant.	—	—	—		
Acting Secretary for Native Affairs -	C. P. Chesnaye	July 4, '98	April 1, '01	Aug 1, '01	500	H
Judge of the High Court	Leicester P. Beaufort, B.C.L. -	June, '01	—	June, '01	1000	H
Secretary	R. A. J. Goode	Oct 20, '00	April 1, '01	July 1, '01	600	H
Chief Clerk -	C. H. Timmler	Jan 1, '99	April 1, '01	Sep 25, '01	400	Q
Clerks -	{ H. C. Parkin	April 24, '99	April 1, '01	May 1, '01	300	Q
	{ D. W. Ferguson	Mar 23, '01	—	Mar 23, '01	275	Q
Junior Assistant	E. Eason -	April 17, '01	—	Nov 1, '01	75	Q & *100
Native Clerk -	1 at £24 p.a.	—	—	—		
Accountant -	T. C. Clark -	Oct 10, '00	—	Oct 10, '00	200	Q & *200
Assistant Accountant	R. Burrow -	Jan 4, '01	April 1, '01	Aug 1, '01	300	Q
Bookkeeper -	W. S. Kinghorn	Aug 24, '01	P	Aug 24, '01	250	Q
Public Works and Transport.						
Foremen -	2 at £275 p.a.	—	—	—		Q
Builders & Artizans	{ 1 at £275 p.a.					Q
	{ 1 at £264 p.a.	—	—	—		
	{ 3 at £240 p.a.					
Conductors and Road Inspectors	{ 1 at £250 p.a.					Q
	{ 1 at £240 p.a.	—	—	—		
	{ 1 at £215 p.a.					
Medical.						
Fort Jameson.						
Principal Medical Officer and District Surgeon	J. C. Spillane, M.B.	June 8, '01	—	June 8, '01	400	H & *100
Abercorn.						
District Surgeon	D. A. Martin, M.R.C.S.	Nov 10, '01	—	Nov 10, '01	400	H & *100
Printing and Stationery.						
Head Printer -	A. E. Crowther	Aug 6, '01	—	Aug 6, '01	300	Q
Native Compositors	2 at £36 p.a.	—	—	—		
Districts and Divisions.						
Fort Jameson.						
Civil Commissioner and Magistrate -	P. H. Selby -	July 1, '98	April 1, '01	Aug 1, '00	600	H
Native Commissioner -	H. Croad -	Oct 16, '94	April 1, '01	April 1, '01	300	Q
Assistant Native Commissioners	{ H. G. Willis -	Oct 18, '00	April 1, '01	Jan 1, '01	275	Q
	{ E. S. B. Tagart	Jan 11, '01	April 1, '01	April 1, '01	250	Q
Probationer -	J. C. Hughes	Aug 11, '01	P	—	225	Q
do. -	J. L. Reid -	Sep 14, '01	P	—	225	Q
Postmaster -	C. T. A. Collard	Mar 29, '01	—	Mar 29, '01	25	Q & *240
Nawalia.						
Native Commissioner	W. E. M. Savage	Oct 1, '00	April 1, '01	Jan 1, '01	275	Q
Petanke.						
Native Commissioner	J. C. C. Coxhead	June 1, '98	April 1, '01	April 1, '01	275	Q
Asst. Nat. Commissioner	P. E. Hall -	Jan 11, '01	April 1, '01	April 1, '01	250	Q
Serenge.						
Native Commissioner	W. P. Kennelly	Jan 1, '00	April 1, '01	April 1, '01	375	Q

* From A.T.T. Company.

Office.	Name.	First.	Fixed.	Present.	Salary.	Allowance.
Kapopo. Native Commissioner	F. E. F. Jones	March, '00	April 1, '01	Jan 1, '01	p. a. 325	Q
M'Kushi. Native Commissioner	J. E. Stephenson	July 1. '00	April 1, '01	Jan 1, '01	275	Q
Feira. Native Commissioner	C. C. Shekleton	Jan 1, '00	April 1, '01	Jan 1. '01	375	Q
Probationer	V. B. Reid	Sep 14, '01	P	—	225	Q
Fife. Civil Commr. & Magistrate	C. McKinnon	Nov 15, '96	April 1, '01	Aug 1, '00	500	H
Native Commissioner	J. H. Forbes	Aug 1, '96	April 1, '01	Jan 1, '01	300	Q
Asst. Nat. Commissioner	R. S. McDonald	Jan 1, '01	April 1, '01	Jan 1, '01	250	Q
Probationer	J. H. West Sheane	Aug 14, '01	P	—	225	Q
Postmaster	S. R. Rothwell	Nov 4, '00	—	Nov 4, '01	25	Q & *240
Mirongo. Native Commissioner	R. Young	May 1, '95	April 1, '01	Jan 1, '01	325	Q
Koka. Supern. Assistant	J. de Jong	Aug 15, '01	—	Aug 15, '01	225	Q
Kasama. Native Commissioner	G. M. E Leyer	Mar 28, '99	April 1, '01	Jan 1, '01	300	Q
Asst. Nat. Commissioner	E. A. A. Jones	July 4, '01	P	Aug 15, '01	225	Q
Mpija. Asst. Nat. Commissioner	P. C. Cookson	Dec 24, '00	April 1, '01	April 1, '01	250	Q
Asst. Nat. Commissioner	F. H. Melland	July 4, '01	P	Aug 15, '01	225	Q
Abercorn. Civil Commr. & Magistrate	H. C. Marshall	June, '95	April 1, '01	Aug 1, '00	500	H
Probationer	H. R. Cox	Sep 11, '01	P	Sep 11, '01	250	Q
Asst. Nat. Commissioner	C. Stevens	Nov 20, '00	April 1, '01	April 1, '01	250	Q
Probationer	J. A. Richards	Oct 28, '01	P	—	225	
Postmaster	J. McNeil	Feb 20, '00	—	Feb 20, '00	25	Q & *240
Sumbu. Native Commissioner	J. L. Greer	Sep 2, '99	April 1, '01	Jan 1, '01	250	Q
Katwe. Native Commissioner	A. C. R. Miller	April 10, '97	April 1, '01	Jan 1, '01	275	Q
Kalungwisi. Civil Commr. & Magistrate	Blair Watson, M.D.	Nov, '91	April 1, '01	Aug 1, '00	500	H
Clerk	S. E. Williams	Dec 1. '00	—	Dec 1, '00	225	Q
Kampanda. Native Commissioner	B. B. Johnstone	April 1, '99	April 1, '01	Jan 1, '01	275	Q
Fort Rosebery. Native Commissioner	H. T. Harrington	Sept 1, '95	April 1, '01	Jan 1, '01	300	Q
Probationer	R. G. Burgess	Sep 14, '01	—	—	225	Q
Mieri Mieri. Native Commissioner	G. G. P. Lyons	Aug 1, '98	April 1, '01	Jan 1, '01	300	Q

* From A.T.T. Company.

Part VI.

LOCAL BOARDS AND COURTS.

LICENSING COURTS.

By the Liquor Regulations, 1895, the Additional Liquor Regulations, 1897, and the Licensing Courts Regulations, 1898, it was provided that Courts for the consideration and determination of applications for, or relating to the granting, renewal or transfer of licences for the sale of intoxicating liquors should be held in and for such Magisterial Districts in Southern Rhodesia as the Administrator may constitute by notice published in the *Government Gazette*. Such Courts are to be held on the first Wednesday in the months of March and September of every year, the Administrator, however, having the power to authorise the holding of a special meeting of any Licensing Court in the event of an emergency requiring that such special meeting should be held.

Each Court so constituted shall consist of the Magistrate of the Division and three members, one of whom shall be nominated by the Administrator, and two by the Municipal Council or Sanitary Board of such town, within such District as the Administrator may designate by notice in the *Gazette*.

In case of an equality of votes in regard to any matter before the Court, the Magistrate shall have a casting vote in addition to a deliberative vote.

The following are the members of each Court for the year 1901-1902 :—

SALISBURY.	A. R. Roberts, Esq.	Government Member.
	H. Philips, Esq.	
	J. Pascoe, Esq.	
UMTALI.	W. Craven, Esq.	Government Member.
	Rudolph Myburgh, Esq.	
	T. Brown, Esq.	
BULAWAYO.	C. T. Holland, Esq.	Government Member.
	J. Kerr, Esq.	
	G. C. Scaer, Esq.	
GWELO.	H. C. Quin, Esq.	Government Member.
	R. W. Brownrigg, Esq.	
	J. J. Campbell, Esq.	

TENDER BOARD.

The Tender Board was established in the year 1897 for the purpose of examining and reporting upon tenders received for the service of the various Government Departments.

The Board consists of five members, who are appointed by the Administrator. The appointments are honorary. The clerical work is performed by a Secretary and an Assistant, who receive £75 and £25 per annum respectively.

Tenders are invited by notice in the *Government Gazette*, and, after examination and consideration, are forwarded with the report and recommendation of the Board to the Administrator, with whom the final decision rests.

The following are the principal services for which tenders are invited:—
Mails; Police, Gaol and Hospital requirements; Building; Printing; and other miscellaneous services.

The following are the Members of the Tender Board :—

> J. H. Kennedy (Chairman).
> H. Ashmead.
> Major P. W. Forbes.
> G. W. Farmaner.
> A. F. Emerton.

> *Secretary*, E. H. Smith Wright.
> *Assistant*, W. H. Orpen.

PERIODICAL COURTS.

Shewing number of Miles from Magistracy, and when holden each month, and also giving names of Issuers of Process.

District.	Where holden.	Miles from Magistracy.	When holden in each month.	Issuer of Process.
Bulawayo ...	Shiloh	28	1st Tuesday	N.C.O., B.S.A.P. in charge
	Inyati	45	1st Thursday	Do. do.
	Mzingwane ...	16	2nd Monday	A. L. Jones
Gwelo ...	Selukwe	25	2nd and 4th Wednesday	Clerk of Court, Gwelo
Tuli ...	Tuli	85	3rd Wednesday	N.C.O., B.S.A.P. in charge

Part VII.

MISCELLANEOUS LISTS.

SPECIAL JUSTICES OF THE PEACE.

In order to provide for the trial of certain offences committed at places distant from the seat of a Magistrate, His Excellency the High Commissioner, on 25th November, 1898, passed certain Regulations for the appointment of Native Commissioners as Special Justices of the Peace, to act within their respective districts, with the powers and jurisdiction conferred by the law of the Cape Colony upon Special Justices of the Peace, and thereupon all the laws of the said Colony with regard to Special Justices of the Peace, the review of their decisions or otherwise shall *mutatis mutandis* apply to the Native Commissioner so appointed. The Native Commissioner shall have and exercise all the powers and jurisdiction conferred upon Resident Magistrates of the said Colony under the provisions of Acts No. 18 of 1873 and No. 7 of 1875 of the said Colony.

In all civil matters between natives, a Native Commissioner who may be appointed a Special Justice of the Peace, shall have the jurisdiction conferred upon Magistrates by the law at the time in force in Southern Rhodesia : provided that it shall be competent for any native to bring any action either before the Special Justice of the Peace or the Magistrate as he may desire.

In civil cases brought by natives in the Court of the Special Justice of the Peace an appeal shall lie to the High Court, as if the case had in the first instance been brought in the Court of the Magistrate of the District.

The following is the list of Special Justices of the Peace :—

Native Commissioner.	*District.*
William Elliot Thomas	... Bulalima and Mangwe.
Donald Harry Moodie	... N'danga.
Archibald Andrew Campbell	... Inseza.
Charles Travers Stuart	... Malima.
Archar Russell Ross ...	... Makoni.
William Edward Edwards Scott	... Hartley.
Ernest Walter Morris	.. Marandellas.
William Edward Farrer	... Sebungwe-Mafungabusi.

REGULATIONS FOR THE INSTRUCTION OF DISTRICT SURGEONS.

General Provisions.†

1. These Regulations shall apply to every District Surgeon, and shall be conformed to as part of the terms of his appointment, except in any case in which special exemption shall be given by the head of the department immediately concerned.

2. The District Surgeon will also be amenable to any Convict and Prisons Regulations framed under the provisions of the Convict Stations and Prisons Management Acts, and in force at the time being. (These Regulations will be found printed in the annexure " A " hereto.)

3. The District Surgeon will be furnished from time to time by the Chief Secretary with copies, in circular form, of any new regulations or instructions bearing on his duty and to which he must conform, that may be issued. He shall file all such communications, together with the instructions provided him on appointment, for future reference and guidance, and on vacating the office of District Surgeon he shall hand such file to his successor in the office.

4. The District Surgeon for the district is required, unless otherwise directed, to reside in the town or village which is the principal seat of magistracy in the district to which he is appointed. In the case of Additional District Surgeons, the place of residence shall be such town or village as shall be determined by the Government. It is not intended to offer hereby any unreasonable obstruction to the District Surgeon's private practice : if, however, that lying beyond the immediate neighbourhood of the place of residence should be such as to prevent him giving the attention to his public duties which is required and may reasonably be expected from him, the matter will have to be brought specially under the consideration of the Government.

It shall be competent for the Government to employ the District Surgeon on any public service in any district contiguous to his own, at the tariff rates attaching to the performance of a like service within the district to which such District Surgeon is specially appointed.

5. During the absence of the District Surgeon from the appointed town or village of residence on his own affairs, whether professional or otherwise, he must make adequate provision, at his own expense, for carrying out any urgent official duty that may arise during his absence : provided that in any case in which a substitute is called in by a Magistrate at the expense of the District Surgeon, such Magistrate shall be required to record in writing his reasons for having employed such a substitute ; but the District Surgeon being allowed

---

† NOTE.—Before these appointments, which are provisional, can be notified in the *Government Gazette*, the officer appointed must signify his assent in writing to the following conditions, and forward the same through th Magistrate for record in the office of the Chief Secretary :—

1. I shall enter upon the duties of District Surgeon at ....with the least possible delay.

2. I have made myself acquainted with the duties required of me, and will acquaint myself with all other directions and instructions which may from time to time be issued relative thereto, and will conform to the same accordingly.

3. If at any time it should be my desire to vacate or resign the said office and my appointment thereto, I agree to apprise the Government of my intention in that respect at least three months previous to the date upon which I will cease to perform the duties of that office.

Signature.......................................

private practice, the Magistrate will, when practicable, cause timely notice to be given to the District Surgeon, when his services are required or are likely to be required on any Government duty, other than mere routine duty, and he will, as far as possible, hold over until the District Surgeon's return any matters which can in his opinion await such return without prejudice to any party concerned, and the District Surgeon should not be detained on any Government duty longer than may be necessary.

The District Surgeon should, however, whenever possible, give early information to the Magistrate of his intention of being absent from the seat of Magistracy for any period over 24 hours.

Whenever the District Surgeon desires to be absent from his District on his own affairs, whether professional or otherwise, for any period over three days, he must apply through the Magistrate for leave of absence, and must provide, to the satisfaction of and at no extra cost to the Government, an efficient substitute to act for him during his absence.

6. During the absence of the District Surgeon on public service, any arrangements which have to be made for carrying out any Government duty that may arise during such absence will not be at the expense of the District Surgeon ; and in this case any fee which may be attached to the performance of the duty will be paid to the person performing such duty. It is, however, open to the District Surgeon to arrange for a substitute, satisfactory to the Government, to perform for him during such absence any duties that may arise, in which case the services of such substitute will, if available, always be obtained, and any fee attaching by virtue of these regulations to any duty so performed will be paid either to the substitute or to the District Surgeon as may be arranged.

7. If during the treatment of any case treated at the Government expense unusual difficulty or danger shall arise. the District Surgeon shall have power to call in, if he deem necessary, additional aid. referring first to the Magistrate for approval, if the case will reasonably admit of the delay necessary for such reference, or if not, reporting as soon as possible that he has done so.

8. Whenever it becomes necessary to obtain the services of any medical practitioner to assist the District Surgeon to perform any operation or to attend any case of assault or sudden injury, or to perform any of the duties of the District Surgeon during his absence on Government duty, or to act for a District Surgeon who is absent on his own affairs, and who shall not have arranged for a substitute to perform his duties, as provided for under regulations numbered 5 and 6 hereof, such medical practitioner shall be paid ten shillings if the visit is between the hours of 6 a.m. and 10 p.m., and twenty shillings if between the hours of 10 p.m. and 6 a.m. : but travelling. operations, and any of the special duties mentioned in the regulations numbered 29 to 39 shall be paid for at the tariff fixed by those regulations. And it shall be the duty of the Magistrate, District Surgeon, member of the Police, or other person so calling in such medical practitioner, to inform him at the time of calling in of the rate of remuneration which he will be entitled to receive.

9. All requests, instructions, &c., from the Magistrate or any responsible officer to the District Surgeon shall be conveyed or confirmed to him in writing.

10. The Magistrate is instructed that any communication forwarded by the District Surgeon to him for transmission to any department should be sent forward in the form in which it is received from the District Surgeon, and not

embodied in a separate letter by the Magistrate, who should, however, invariably in the covering letter forwarding such communication, report upon the subject matter of such communication ; a copy, however of the communication should be preserved in the Magistrate's office, and a copy also of any reply to such communication should be furnished to the District Surgeon as soon as received by the Magistrate.

11. If any reasonable direction or recommendation duly conveyed (whenever possible in writing) by the District Surgeon to a responsible officer is not attended to, the District Surgeon shall notify the fact in writing to the Magistrate, and if thereafter such direction or recommendation still remains neglected, then directly to the Secretary to the Law Department.

12. The District Surgeon is not empowered to order the admission of any person requiring medical treatment into any gaol or gaol ward or hospital, but should he deem it to be urgently and imperatively necessary that any pauper or helpless person whom, in his official capacity, he has been called upon to attend, should be admitted for treatment to the gaol or gaol hospital, there being no other hospital or place available, he should at once report the circumstance to the Magistrate, or his substitute, who is empowered to authorise the admission, if he deem fit. Under no circumstances, however, will the admission into a gaol or gaol hospital be sanctioned of any person, not a prisoner, suffering from infectious or contagious disease.

Duties of the District Surgeon.

13. Subject to the payment of such special fees and allowances as are provided for by regulations numbered 29 to 39 hereof, the District Surgeon will be required to undertake all or any of the following duties free of charge :—

14. He will be required to conform to and carry out any prison regulations at the time being in force relating to the duties of medical officers of gaols.

15. He will attend every inquest when required so to do by the Magistrate, or other competent officer holding an enquiry.

16. He will be required to make an inspection within the scope of his professional capacity, and furnish a report thereon as the Administrator may from time to time direct. He is also required to furnish annually and at such other times as the Administrator may deem necessary, a report upon the prevalence of infectious or contagious diseases in, or the state of the public health and sanitation of his district, and upon any matters relating thereto ; and he shall for this purpose keep all such records as may be prescribed by the Administrator from time to time ; and every such record shall be and remain the property of the Government, and shall at all times be open to or be delivered to the Magistrate or other person appointed thereto by the Government, and on the District Surgeon vacating his office shall be handed, duly posted up to date, to his successor in the office.

He shall also, when required, furnish reports on any matter coming within his official knowledge as District Surgeon, and he shall give his written opinion when the same may be officially required by any Court or by the Magistrate of the district, on any professional subject or on any question connected with the public welfare or the administration of justice.

17. He shall keep registers in such form as the Government may from time to time prescribe, of all cases medically treated by him in the discharge of his duty as District Surgeon, and of all public vaccinations and medico-legal duties performed by him : and every such register shall be and remain the property of the Government, and shall at all times be open to the use or inspection of the Magistrate or other person appointed by the Government thereto, and on vacating the office of District Surgeon shall be handed, duly posted up to date, to his successor in the office.

18. He will have the medical care of prisoners in the gaol or gaols he is required to visit, and of paupers, lunatics, and lepers maintained by or drawing relief from Government in his district other than in a public asylum, and he will have, when required, to certify as to the physical condition of any pauper and his or her capacity for earning a livelihood, for which purpose he shall, whenever possible, avail himself of visits to the neighbourhood in which any pauper may dwell to inspect such pauper's condition.

19. He shall give professional advice and treatment gratis to the Police, Gaol officials, and to such Postal and Telegraphic officials as the Government may from time to time direct, residing or stationed in the town within which he himself resides, as well as to their wives and families (midwifery cases excepted), and to prisoners and to paupers : the term pauper being taken to mean persons who are in a state of absolute poverty, and physically incapable of earning a livelihood, and who have no relatives or friends in sufficiently affluent circumstances willing to provide for their subsistence, it not being the intention to defray from the public funds the cost of medical advice, attendance or medicine supplied to those who are in a position to pay for the same.

20. He will be required to examine all paupers, lepers, or lunatics, before they are sent from country districts to a hospital ; it being an instruction to the Magistrate that no such person shall be so forwarded unless the District Surgeon certifies in writing that he is able to undertake the journey.

21. In cases of accident or assault the District Surgeon must examine and, if necessary attend to, when called upon to do so by the Magistrate, Assistant Magistrate, or any judicial officer or member of the Police, whether at the time in uniform or not, any injured person, and report in writing the nature of the injuries from which he (or she) is suffering.

The Government will, however, offer no objection to the District Surgeon or a medical practitioner, as the case may be, who has been summoned by the Magistrate or Police to attend any person, receiving from such person the customary fees for his services ; but in the event of any fee being recovered from such person, no payment on account of such services will then be made by the Government to the District Surgeon or medical practitioner recovering such fee.

22. He shall perform generally all medico-legal duties arising in his district, including the performance of Post Mortems required under " The Inquest Act."

23. He shall carry out all the provisions relating to District Surgeons of Part II. of the " Contagious Diseases Prevention Act, 1885," and shall give medical attendance in his official capacity of District Surgeon to all persons suffering from " contagious disease " as the Magistrate shall authorise in that behalf, and shall not make to any such person, if a pauper, any charge for such attendance.

24. He shall perform public vaccination whenever and wherever required to do so by the Government or Magistrate, and shall not wilfully fail to attend for this purpose at any duly appointed centre or station at the duly appointed hour.

25. He shall, when required, examine and report on recruits for the Mashonaland and Matabeleland Constabularly or other similar police force, and on the health of such other candidates for the Public Service as the Government may from time to time prescribe.

26. He shall attend, free of charge, any member of the British South Africa Police in his district when called on to do so.

27. He shall perform free of charge such casual duties as the Government may from time to time require.

28. He will carry out any duties devolving upon District Surgeons under the provisions of any Ordinance now or at the time being in force within these territories.

Special Allowances and Fees.

29. In addition to such annual allowance as the District Surgeon may receive under the terms of his appointment, he is entitled to the following special fees and allowances for the performance of the respective duties hereinafter set forth.

30. *Certification of Lunatics.*—District Surgeons, Government Medical Officers (other than Medical Officers of Lunatic Asylums acting in the discharge of the ordinary duties of their office), and medical practitioners are entitled to be paid a fee of two guineas (£2 2s.) for every certificate, whether of lunacy or of mental soundness, granted by them.

In addition to this fee every District Surgeon, Government Medical Officer and medical practitioner as aforesaid, if summoned to appear before any person or court to testify on oath touching any matter respecting which the said Act provides that inquiry may be instituted, will be entitled to be paid his expenses as if he were summoned to attend as a witness upon a trial in a criminal case.

31. *Examination and Certification of Lepers.*—Every District Surgeon or Medical Officer who, after examination of a person suspected of leprosy, is satisfied that such person is a leper, shall be required to furnish a certificate of leprosy in terms of Section 5 of the "Leprosy Repression Act, 1884."

A fee of one guinea shall be payable for the certificate so furnished in respect of each such leper.

This fee will be payable whether or not the person is found on examination by the District Surgeon or Medical Officer to be a leper.

32. *Treatment of Paupers under the provisions of the Contagious Diseases Prevention Act.*—The District Surgeon will (unless in special cases some other rate of remuneration shall be fixed) be paid for the medical treatment of persons authorised in the manner provided by Regulation No. 23 hereof, under the provisions of Part II. of "The Contagious Diseases Prevention Act, 1885," an allowance at the rate of fifteen shillings per patient for each month or portion of a month during which he is under treatment, when the number does not exceed ten; if beyond that number, he shall be paid ten shillings per patient for each month or portion of a month.

A month shall be taken to be the period included between the corresponding dates in any two consecutive calendar months.

33. *Allowance in respect of Prisoners and Paupers.*—Medical Officers of gaols shall be entitled to the following allowance in respect of the undermentioned matter:—

> For every confinement of a prisoner attended by him in gaol, or of a pauper, when authorised in writing by the Magistrate to give such attendance, a fee of   £3   3   0

34. *Allowance for supply of Medicines.*—For providing all necessary medicines for the treatment of Gaol Officials, Mashonaland or Matabeleland Constabulary, and B.S.A. Police, and such other Government Officials as the Government may require to be attended, with their wives and families, and who are not inmates of a hospital, one shilling per patient per day during the time the patient is under treatment, or such other allowance as may from time to time be fixed by the Government. The District Surgeon shall in every case record in a book kept for that purpose the nature of the medicine and the amount of it provided.

35. *Operations.*—The District Surgeon shall be entitled to the following scale of fees for the performance of the operations and services (including subsequent treatment) enumerated below, in respect of any pauper, prisoner or public servant to whom the District Surgeon is required by these Regulations to gratuitously give aid:—

> For treatment of compound fracture or compound dislocation of the thigh, knee, or shoulder ; amputation of leg, arm, foot or hand ; ligature of the great arteries ; abscission of the breast: abdominal section ; or trephining the skull £3   3   0

> For treatment of simple dislocation of the shoulder, knee or hip ; compound fracture of arm or leg ; simple fracture of thigh ; operation for strangulated hernia ; laryngotomy or tracheotomy   ...   2   2   0

> For treatment of simple fracture or dislocation of the arm, leg, ribs, clavicle, patella, ankle, wrist or jaw ; amputation of fingers or toes ; surgical puncture of bladder, chest or abdomen ; the operation for fistula or hæmorrhoids, the administration of an anæsthetic for, or rendering necessary professional assistance to a District Surgeon in the performance of any of the before-mentioned operations   ...   1   1   0

If several of the foregoing fees specified become payable with respect to the same person at the same time, or in consequence of the same cause or injury, the District Surgeon shall be entitled only to one of such fees, and if unequal, to the highest.

In any surgical case not provided for in the above tariff, which has presented peculiar difficulty, or required and received long attendance from the District Surgeon, the Government will make such reasonable extra allowances as it may think fit.

In every case the District Surgeon will be required to furnish a certificate that the operation was necessarily undertaken.

36. *Performance of Post Mortems and giving evidence at Inquests.*—District Surgeons and medical practitioners are entitled to the following fees for Inquest services rendered under the provisions of "The Inquest Act of 1875":—

(1) For examination of dead body or supposed human remains (including opening of the cranium and the examination of the viscera) with medical certificate as to post mortem appearances and cause of death   £2   2   0

(2) For travelling, and for detention while giving evidence before any inquest, the fees provided by Regulations Nos. 38 and 39 hereof.

37. *Other Fees.*—District Surgeons and medical practitioners shall be allowed the subjoined tariff of fees for the following services performed at the request of the Magistrate:—

(1) Examination of dead body where it is unnecessary to dissect, with medical certificate as to post mortem appearances and cause of death   ...   £1   1   0

(2) For examination of a person bodily injured or in a state of assumed or presumed insanity, or of apparently feigned sickness, with medical certificate   1   1   0

(3) For examinations of recruits and others, under Regulation 25, each   0   5   0

38. *Allowance while Travelling.*—For every journey taken on service, other than that of giving evidence in a Court of Law, when the distance travelled exceeds three miles from the offices of the Magistrate, or in the case of there being no such offices, then from the centre of the town or village in which the District Surgeon resides, the District Surgeon shall be paid an allowance at the rate of ten shillings per hour (each hour to be reckoned as five miles) for the whole distance travelled, both going and returning, but the allowance, including detention, is in no case to exceed three pounds.

When the journey cannot reasonably be performed on horseback, the District Surgeon shall be provided with a conveyance at the Government cost.

For journeys taken for the purpose of giving evidence in a Court of Justice, or at any inquest or other judicial enquiry, District Surgeons and Government Medical Officers shall be paid, when the distance travelled exceeds three miles from the seat of the Court or the place of enquiry, at the rate of ten shillings per hour (each hour to be reckoned as five miles) for the whole distance travelled, both going and returning, between—in the case of the District Surgeon, the seat of Magistracy, or, in the case of any Medical Officer or a District Surgeon not residing at the seat of Magistracy, his usual residence and the seat of the Court or place of enquiry. Provided that if the greater part of the mileage may be performed by rail or coach, then the travelling

---

† EXAMPLE.—Thus, supposing the residence of the Medical Officer to be seven miles from the Railway Station, and that the journey by rail to the seat of the Court occupies one hour, the allowance for travelling would be calculated thus:—

Fourteen miles to and fro by road, three hours ..   £1 10   0
One hour by rail each way, two hours   ...   1   0   0

Total allowance for travelling   ...   £2 10   0

allowance for the portion of the journey by rail or coach must be calculated according to the time actually occupied by the train or coach in traversing the distance,† together with any time necessarily or actually occupied in waiting for the next available train or coach to return after the taking of the evidence of the District Surgeon or Medical Officer by the Court: this includes necessary detention occasioned by changing trains during the journey.

Portions of an hour, after adding together the entire time occupied in a journey there and back, shall be reckoned as a whole hour.

39. *Detention.*—District Surgeons will under no circumstances be paid any allowance for detention while on service, except in the following special cases:—

(a) *Detention as Professional Witness.*—District Surgeons and Government Medical Officers will be paid at the rate of seven shillings and sixpence per hour for detention while in necessary attendance as professional witnesses before any Court of Law, but the maximum payment shall not exceed three pounds sterling for any one day's attendance.

A certificate stating the number of hours' detention, and that the officer attended in his professional capacity, will in each case be required.

(b) *Night Detention.*—Whenever it shall be impossible for the District Surgeon, setting out before 8 o'clock a.m., and thereafter exercising due despatch, to travel to his destination, perform the service required of him, and return home before 8 o'clock p.m. of the same day, he shall be entitled to an allowance of fifteen shillings for the night's detention.

A certificate stating the time when the District Surgeon set out and arrived back, the number of miles travelled to his destination and back, the time actually and necessarily engaged in the performance of his official duty, and that all reasonable despatch was employed, will be required in each case.

(c) *Detention while performing Public Vaccination.*—The District Surgeon will be paid for reasonable detention at the rate of ten shillings per hour, while actually, solely, and necessarily engaged in the performance of gratuitous vaccination at any appointed centre within the district, except at the seat of Magistracy or other authorised headquarters of the District Surgeon.

A certificate stating the number of hours the District Surgeon was necessarily detained in the sole performance of gratuitous vaccination, and the number of persons actually vaccinated during such time, will in every case be required.

No allowance will be paid for detention unless all available means are actively taken by the District Surgeon to vaccinate as many persons as possible.

All Government Officers shall afford the District Surgeon, when engaged in vaccinating, every reasonable assistance in carrying out this duty.

ANNEXURE A.

Prison Regulations applying to the District Surgeon in his capacity of Medical Officer to the Gaol, framed under the Provisions of the " Convict Stations and Prisons Management Act, 1888," and of the " Convict Stations and Prisons Management, 1888, Amendment Ordinance, 1893."

1. The Medical Officer shall keep all such books and records as may from time to time be prescribed by the Attorney General.

2. He shall inspect the whole of the prison, including the bedding, wards, cells, latrines and urinals at least once in every week, and at such other times as the Magistrate may in writing direct, and he shall briefly record in a book to be kept for that purpose the state as regards sanitation and general cleanliness in which, at the time of the inspection, he found the prison and all connected therewith, and he shall, whenever he deems necessary, or when he may be required to do so, furnish to the Magistrate a report in writing on the sanitary state of the prison and the health of the prisoners.

3. He shall at least once in each week, and, as far as possible, at irregular intervals, inspect the quality of the food, cooked and uncooked, supplied to the prisoners, and shall report in writing should he be of opinion that any article of food is unwholesome or of indifferent or inferior quality.

4. He shall visit the gaol at least twice in each week and shall see every prisoner confined in gaol at least once in each week, and, as far as possible, ascertain the state of health of every prisoner at the time of his admission to the gaol or before he is put to hard labour. He shall see every sick prisoner at least once a day, and shall certify in writing whether such are fit for labour.

If the Attorney General shall deem it advisable that any gaol, owing to its importance, the class of its prisoners, or any other circumstances, shall be visited daily by the Medical Officer, he shall issue an instruction requiring the Medical Officer to visit such gaol regularly at least once a day.

5. Subject to the following reservations, he shall vaccinate every prisoner as soon as possible after his reception into the gaol, *i.e.*, unless :

(a) There be an official record that vaccination has been properly performed, either (1) before being sent from some other gaol or convict station, or (2) on some previous conviction, not exceeding in any case seven years back ; or

(b) He is able to certify either (1) that the prisoner is not in a fit state of health to submit to vaccination, or (2) that if vaccination be performed the prisoner (if under order for removal) will not be in a fit condition to travel to another gaol or station on the specified date (to be named in the certificate).

6. He shall by written order direct such modifications of labour, clothing, bedding, diet, or treatment as in particular cases he may deem necessary.

7. He shall at once report in writing to the Magistrate on the proper form, the case of any prisoner to which he may think it necessary on medical grounds to draw attention, and shall make such recommendation as he may deem proper, and he shall similarly report when the condition of any sick prisoner appears to assume an aspect of danger.

8. He shall immediately report in writing to the Magistrate, in order that it may be communicated to the Secretary to the Law Department, whenever he shall be of opinion :

(a) That the mind of any prisoner is affected, or
(b) That the life of any prisoner will be endangered or his health affected by his continuance in prison, or
(c) That his health requires his removal to some other station, or
(d) That the prisoner will not survive his sentence, or
(e) That he is totally unfit for prison discipline ; giving in each case the grounds of his opinion.

9. He shall in every instance of alleged pregnancy in a female prisoner under sentence, satisfy himself thoroughly that pregnancy really exists, and in the event of such being the condition, to report on the following points :—

(a) The date on which labour may be expected to supervene, and the date of expiration of the sentence.
(b) Whether it is possible for the prisoner to be delivered in the gaol with safety.
(c) Whether retention in gaol is likely to lead to premature labour, or to endanger the life of either the mother or the offspring, and, if so, by what means.

10. He shall be required to carefully examine every prisoner under sentence before his removal to any other prison or convict station, and to certify (if able) that such prisoner is free from any contagious or infectious disease, in good health, fit to travel, and not subject to any malady or defect, or mental or physical infirmity caused by old age or otherwise, which would prevent him from having the full use of his limbs, or in any way interfere with his being put to ordinary hard labour. And if unable to grant such certificate, then he shall certify the reasons which prevent him from doing so.

No examination made under this regulation shall be deemed complete unless it includes an examination of the heart, lungs, urine and temperature of the prisoner, as well as his powers of sight and hearing. The Medical Officer should also ascertain how the journey is to be made, and if on foot he should state the maximum distance which the prisoner can safely be made to march during each day.

11. Whenever he shall find or suspect a prisoner or an official, or any member of an official's family, or any inmate of or visitor to the prison to be suffering from any infectious or contagious disease, he shall report the circumstance to the Gaoler and give all necessary instructions in writing for the prompt segregation of the patient, and for preventing the spread of such infectious or contagious disease, and he shall forthwith report the fact, together with any circumstance bearing on it, in writing to the Magistrate, stating if possible the cause of the disease. Whenever illness arises from any preventable cause and the Medical Officer's written representations are not attended to with reasonable despatch, he shall notify the omission direct to the Secretary to the Law Department.

12. If any case of peculiar difficulty or danger should occur, the Medical Officer shall have the power to call in additional aid, referring previously to the Secretary to the Law Department, through the Magistrate, for approval, if the case shall reasonably admit of such reference. No serious operation shall be

performed without a previous consultation with another medical practitioner except under very urgent circumstances not admitting of delay, which circumstances the Medical Officer shall record in his Journal.

13. In every case of death of a prisoner he shall, as soon after death as possible, hold an autopsy of the body, unless the Secretary to the Law Department shall on application in any particular case permit such examination to be dispensed with, and he shall duly record, and certify thereto upon the form provided, the results of such examination, together with, in his opinion, the true cause of death.

14. In the case of a prisoner sentenced to spare diet or to undergo solitary confinement in cells, he shall, on receipt of written notice from the Gaoler, examine and certify as to his fitness to undergo such punishment.

15. He shall attend the infliction of all corporal punishments at the proper hour, of which he shall receive written notice from the Gaoler. He shall examine the prisoner carefully before he is flogged ; and shall, having regard to Regulation 118 of the Prison Regulations, 1899, and to any circumstance which may in his judgment demand consideration, give such directions in writing as he may deem necessary. If he consider that the prisoner is in a fit state to undergo the punishment, he shall give a certificate to that effect to the Gaoler. In cases in which he may direct that the punishment should not be carried out, or only partially carried out, he shall inform the Gaoler and report his reasons for such direction in writing to the Magistrate.

16. He shall attend at every execution of the sentence of capital punishment, and shall as soon thereafter as may be, make a careful post-mortem examination of the body. He shall certify to the Sheriff, Deputy Sheriff, or other officer charged with carrying out such execution, the fact that life is extinct. The body shall not be removed until such certificate is given.

17. He shall record in writing all directions given by him to the Gaoler pursuant to these regulations, and if any direction or recommendation conveyed by him in writing to any responsible officer is not carried out, he shall notify the fact to the Magistrate ; and if his recommendations are still disregarded, then to the Secretary to the Law Department.

VACCINATION.

The subjoined Regulations framed under Section 53 of the Public Health Act, 1883, are in operation in this country. (Government Notice 208 of 1898.)

1. Every District Surgeon and Vaccinator is required to vaccinate gratuitously :—

    (1) Any child under the age of fourteen years whose parents are, in his opinion, unable to pay the customary fee.

    (2) Any child under the age of fourteen years whose parents or the person having custody of such child shall produce a certificate from any Justice of the Peace in the district, stating that the parents of such child are, or in the case of an orphan that such orphan is, in indigent circumstances and that such child ought to be vaccinated gratuitously.

    (3) Any person whom the Magistrate may, in writing, direct to be vaccinated gratuitously.

2. Every District Surgeon shall, when required to do so by the Magistrate of the district, proceed to the different districts in order to vaccinate such per sons as may desire to be vaccinated, or whom such Surgeon may be required to vaccinate gratuitously. A District Surgeon should not be sent on a vaccinating tour without the previous sanction of the Administrator. District Surgeons should be paid at tariff rates for actual distance travelled, and shall not be entitled to any allowance for detention.

3. The Magistrate and Civil Commissioner shall cause timely notice to be given of the date appointed for the visits of the District Surgeon, and of the place appointed in each district for his attendance for the performance of vaccination.

4. District Surgeons should take care to maintain at all times a sufficient supply of good vaccine lymph, which can be obtained from the Medical Director, Salisbury.

LIST OF DISTRICT SURGEONS.

Salisbury : Thos. Stewart, M.B., C.M. (Glas.), £360.
Bulawayo : H. L. Smith, M.B. (Dub.), £500 ; £100 quarters.
Gwelo : H. K. Smyth, M.B., B.Ch., B.A.I., £275.
Umtali : W. Craven, M.R.C.S., L.R.C.P., £275.
Victoria : M. J. Williams, M.R.C.S., L.R.C.P., £275.
Hartley : W. H. Eaton, M.B., C.M. (Edin.), £275.
Melsetter : G. B. D. Macdonald, M.B., C.M. (Aberd.), £375.
Enkeldoorn : A. D. Owen, M.R.C.S., L.R.C.P., £275.
Gwanda : H. Roscoe, M.R.C.S., L.R.C.P., £275.
Selukwe : A. W. Forrester, L.R.C.P., L.R.C.S , £275.
Belingwe : F. M. Morris, M.B. (Lond.), M.R.C.S., L.R.C.P., £275.

Part VIII.

SOUTHERN RHODESIA CIVIL SERVICE RULES AND REGULATIONS.

————

Regulations to Establish and Define the Civil Service of Rhodesia.

1. The Civil Service of Rhodesia shall include and consist of all persons appointed by the Administrator who are continuously employed in the discharge of duties, other than purely police or military, in any Department of the Public Service, not being Judges of the High Court or members of the personal staff of the Administrator.

PROVIDED:

(a) That such persons are not remunerated solely by fees or allowances.

(b) That their whole time is devoted to the Public Service, except in cases of the holders of such offices as the Administrator may from time to time determine.

(c) That nothing in these Regulations contained shall affect or interfere with the provisions of the High Commissioner's Proclamation No. 22 of 1896, or with the powers of control exercised by the High Commissioner as therein set forth.

2. The fixed establishment of the Civil Service as above defined shall consist of :—

(a) Every person who may be appointed to any office mentioned in the Schedule A to these Regulations, excepting a person holding office on probation, or appointed temporarily, or for a term of months or years to any office.

(b) Every person holding, or who may hereafter be appointed to any office which the Administrator may place in such schedule.

(c) Every other person engaged in the discharge of duties not of a purely temporary character, who on the completion of at least six years' continuous service shall obtain from the Head of his Department a certificate of efficiency and good conduct.

3, The words "Head of Department" in these Regulations and in the Rules and Regulations framed thereunder, shall be taken to mean the member of the Council for the time controlling or representing the Department to which any person is appointed, or in which he is serving.

4. Whenever it becomes necessary to admit a person into the Civil Service to fill any office included in Schedule A to these Regulations, which may be vacant, the Head of the Department shall submit the name of the person, in his opinion, best fitted to fill the office for appointment on probation.

5. The person so appointed on probation shall not be placed on the fixed establishment until he shall have served on probation for a period of at least twelve months, and until he shall have received a certificate signed by some officer specified in Schedule A, under whom he shall have directly served, attesting his fitness to be permanently employed, and that his conduct and diligence during probation have been satisfactory.

6. No person shall continue to serve on probation for more than eighteen months, and should any person fail within eighteen months to obtain the requisite certificate of his fitness to be permanently employed, the Administrator shall decide whether such person is unfit for service generally, or shall be allowed a further trial for not exceeding twelve months in the same or another department.

7. At any time during the period of probation of any person, it shall be lawful for the Administrator, with or without notice, to remove him from the Service.

8. The Administrator may appoint to any office not included in Schedule A to these Regulations, such persons as may be necessary for the efficient conduct of the Public Service, and if at any time the Administrator shall deem it expedient in the interests of the Public Service to dispense with the services of any person so appointed, not being a person on the fixed establishment, he shall be at liberty to do so with or without notice.

9. It shall be lawful for the Administrator from time to time to make, add to, amend or repeal rules providing for : —

(a) Appointment of officers.
(b) The efficient performance of their duties by all officers and the maintenance of discipline.
(c) The grades, classification, conditions of promotion, duties, hours of attendance and leave of officers.
(d) The grant of retiring allowances to officers, and of pensions to their widows.
(e) The establishment, working and management of pensions and guarantee funds.
(f) All other matters connected with the Public Service.

The Administrator may for any offence or for violation of any duty prescribed by such Rules, provide penalties for the punishment of offenders by way of reprimand, fine, deprivation, or reduction of salary or emoluments, reduction in rank, suspension for a period, fixed or indefinite, enforced resignation or dismissal.

10. If any officer on the fixed establishment be guilty of any breach of such Rules, such officer may be suspended by the Head of the Department pending enquiry into such breach.

11. No person who is proved to the satisfaction of the Administrator to be habitually using intoxicating liquors to excess shall be retained in the Civil Service.

12. If any officer be convicted of any crime and sentenced to imprisonment without the option of a fine, or become insolvent, or be imprisoned for debt, or be proved to be so addicted to the use of intoxicating liquors as to be frequently unfit for the performance of his duties, he shall be deemed to have forfeited his office and thereupon cease to perform his duties or receive his salary, and pending any enquiry under this section as to any officer, the Head of the Department may suspend him from office upon such conditions as he may deem just.

13. When any officer has forfeited his office by reason of becoming insolvent or being imprisoned for debt, if he prove to the satisfaction of the Administrator that his insolvency or imprisonment has not been caused or attended by any fraud, extravagance, or dishonourable conduct, the Administrator may reinstate such officer in his former position, or place him in some other, if he be in other respects fit for the performance of the requisite duties and able to undertake them.

14. The several Departments of the Civil Service shall be considered and treated as one Service, and every person serving therein shall be liable at any time to be transferred or removed by the Administrator from one office or Department to another, and from one station to another, on promotion or otherwise; and when so transferred or removed, except at his own request, the reasonable travelling expenses of himself and family shall be paid on production of proper vouchers: provided that no person, unless disrated in accordance with such rules as aforesaid, shall be transferred without his own consent to an office of a lower grade, or one to which a lower salary, including allowances capable of being calculated for pension purposes, is attached.

15. Any officer on the fixed establishment who may desire to resign his appointment shall be required to give such notice, not exceeding three months of his intention so to do, as the Head of the Department may require, and any officer leaving the Service without having given such notice, shall forfeit such sum not exceeding three months' salary, as the Administrator may determine.

16. From and after the 1st July, 1898, it shall not be lawful to appoint to any office of Magistrate or Assistant Magistrate any person who on that date had not served five years or upwards in the service of the Company, unless he shall have passed the Civil Service Law Examination of the Cape Colony, or some other law examination approved by the Administrator.

17. In the working and interpretation of these Regulations, and of the Rules and Regulations framed thereunder, reference shall be made to the Civil Service Acts, Rules and Regulations of the *Cape Colony, and in all cases not provided for the Administrator may follow the provisions of the said Cape Acts, Rules and Regulations.

18. These Regulations may be cited as the "Civil Service of Rhodesia Regulations, 1898."

SCHEDULE.

Chief Secretary.
Under Secretary.
Secretary to Deputy Administrator.

Chief Accountant.
Auditor.
Postmaster-General.
Secretary for Native Affairs.
Chief Native Commissioners, Mashonaland and Matabeleland.
Attorney-General.
Solicitor-General.
Secretary to Law Department.
Master and Registrar of High Court.
Assistant Registrar of High Court.
Registrar of Deeds.
Civil Commissioners and Magistrates.
Commissioner of Mines and Public Works.
Assistant Commissioner of Mines and Public Works.
Chief Inspector of Public Works, Salisbury.
Surveyor-General.
Collector of Customs.
Assistant Surveyor General and Examiner of Diagrams.
Secretaries, Accountants, Clerks, and Examiners of Accounts in the Departments of the foregoing.
Agent in Capetown.
Inspector of Public Works, Matabeleland.
Postmasters whose whole time is given to official duties, Inspectors, Telegraphists and Assistants in Post Office, not in temporary employment.

RULES AND REGULATIONS OF THE CIVIL SERVICE OF RHODESIA.

I.—APPOINTMENTS.

1. No person shall receive an appointment in the Civil Service
(a) Unless he has attained the age of 18 years.
(b) Unless he shall pass a medical examination by a medical officer approved by the Administrator, and shall receive a certificate to the effect that he is free from any physical or mental disease or defect likely to interfere with the efficient discharge of his duties.
(c) Unless he is of good character and temperate habits, and free from any legal disability.

II.—HOURS OF ATTENDANCE.

2. The ordinary hours of attendance to be observed in the Public Offices shall be at the least from 9 a.m. to 4 p.m., and on Saturdays from 9 a.m. to 1 p.m.

The Permanent Head or the Chief Clerk of each department of office will be charged with the duty of seeing that these hours are regularly observed by all officers. All officers shall attend at their offices for such longer period as may from time to time be ordered or required.

All officers will be required to devote themselves during the hours of attendance exclusively to the discharge of their public duties.

III.—LEAVE OF ABSENCE.

3. Subject to the exigencies of the Service, officers to whom these rules are applicable, are not ordinarily expected to attend at their respective offices for the discharge of their ordinary duties on the following Public Holidays, viz. :— New Year's Day, Good Friday, Easter Monday, Whit Monday, Queen's Birthday, Christmas Day and the day following, Occupation Days—Mashonaland and Matabeleland, and Shangani Day.

4. Subject to the exigencies of the Service, vacation leave of seven weeks in every year may be granted on full pay to any officer to whom these rules are applicable, after the completion of one year's continuous public service, upon his making adequate and satisfactory provision for the due performance of the duties of his office without extra cost to the public, and any such officer of less than one year's service may, on special application, obtain not exceeding fourteen day's leave on the same conditions.

5. Should it appear that an officer would be practically debarred from obtaining any vacation leave of absence by the operation of the preceding rule, requiring that adequate and satisfactory provision must be made for the due performance of his duties during his absence on leave, without extra cost to the public, the Administrator may, in such case, relax the rule to any extent he may think proper, by directing that the whole or any portion of the cost entailed by such leave may be defrayed out of the public revenue.

6. At any time after the expiration of three and a half years' continuous service, any officer may obtain vacation leave of absence for the purpose of visiting some place beyond the Company's Territories, on the conditions mentioned in paragraph 7 hereof, for a period not exceeding the excess of the total vacation leave which might have been granted to him during the preceding four or lesser number of years, counting the year in which the leave falls, over the aggregate of the periods of leave, if any, which have actually been granted to him during the same years under the preceding paragraphs : provided that in no case shall vacation leave be granted for a longer period than seven months.   The calculation shall be made on a lesser number of years than four when to the advantage of the applicant, and all leave without pay shall be excluded from such calculation.

7. Any officer to whom vacation leave is granted under the preceding paragraphs shall not receive full salary within any period of three years for more than five months of his absence from his duties, and shall receive half salary during the remainder of his absence : but if he shall have had no leave of absence during the preceding six months, and not more than four weeks' leave of absence within the preceding three and a half years, he may obtain five months' leave of absence on full pay : provided that an officer entitled to seven weeks' leave may, notwithstanding this rule, obtain such leave on full pay, subject to the provisions of paragraph 4, at any time after the expiration of twelve months from the termination of long leave under the preceding paragraph.

8. In case any officer to whom leave is granted occupies quarters owned or rented by Government, he shall be entitled to occupy them during such time as he may be on leave on full or half pay, unless, in the opinion of the Head of the Department, it is essential for the performance of the duties of the office

that the "locum tenens" should reside in the quarters, in which case the officer on leave shall be required to vacate the whole or part of such quarters as may be necessary.

9. As a rule, emoluments which do not count for pension may not be drawn by any officer on leave : provided that a local allowance may be treated as ordinary salary with the special sanction of the Head of the Department.

10. In all cases in which any officer on leave shall be receiving less than his full salary and emoluments, the amount deducted shall be available to cover the cost of the performance of his duties during his absence.

11. Subject to the exigencies of the Service, and to such instructions, if any, as may be issued from time to time by the Head of the Department, any Chief of an office may take or grant to officers in his Department occasional leave of absence, not exceeding three days at a time. A return of all leave so granted shall be forwarded to the Head of the Department every month in case of large, and every quarter in the case of small Departments.

12. Special leave of absence may be granted by the Administrator to any officer, irrespective of his length of service, in cases of serious indisposition, or of urgent private affairs, if it shall be proved that such indulgence is absolutely necessary.

13. In cases of "serious indisposition" it must be certified, to the satisfaction of the Administrator, by one or more medical practitioners, approved of by the Head of the Department, that the state of the officer's health renders the leave absolutely necessary.

14. In cases of "urgent private affairs," the nature of such urgent affairs must be stated to the Head of the Department.

15. When special leave is granted in cases of "serious indisposition," the period (including any vacation leave granted within the preceding two years) shall not exceed nine months, and the person obtaining such leave may receive such salary, during his absence from his duties, as may be determined by the Administrator, provided that he shall not receive full salary for a longer period than seven months, within any period of two years, or more than half salary for the remainder of such leave.

16. When special leave of absence is granted on the ground of "urgent private affairs," any ordinary vacation leave which may be granted may be extended on the same conditions by a period not exceeding three months, during which additional period the person may receive half salary.

17. Subject to the exigencies of the Service, special leave may be granted to any person who shall make application therefor upon condition that he shall not draw any salary during his absence from his duties.

18. All leave of absence granted to any officer shall be recorded in a convenient form in the department to which he belongs, and with the exception of leave granted under paragraph 11 hereof, it shall also be recorded in the "Leave" Register kept in the office of the Chief Secretary.

15. As soon as any officer in charge of a department or sub-department resumes duty after leave of absence, the fact shall be reported to the Head of the Department.

20. Every application for leave of absence, other than for leave under paragraph 15 hereof, must be made on the form prescribed for the purpose— vide annexures—and all instructions on such forms must be carefully complied with.

ANNEXURE 1.

Form of Application for Leave of Absence.

Name of Applicant..

Office or Situation and Station........................ ....

Length of Continuous Service... . ...

Emoluments of Office in detail :—

    Salary... ....

    Local Allowance.. .. ..

    Quarters or House Allowance............... ....

    Rations or Ration Allowance.................... ....

Leave during preceding four years	189	..................days ;
each ending on the day of the month	189	..................days ;
on which it is proposed that the leave	190	..................days ;
shall commence.	190	..................days ;

Length of leave asked for................   From......... ....

months....................days   ...   To.... ....

On what terms in respect to Salary and Emoluments... ....

Whether on the ground of serious indisposition*............................ .....

               or on Urgent Affairs..

               or as ordinary Vacation Leave.................................

Arrangements for the discharge of Applicant's duties during his absence on

    leave..

Applicant's address during his absence on leave ....

Where he wishes to draw his pay during leave..

        To be signed by the Head of
        Department.

....Office.

...................................190 .   Approved................................

   *A medical certificate, signed by one or more medical practitioners approved of by the Head of the Department, is required, and it must be shown that leave is absolutely necessary.

ANNEXURE 2.

(a) Name and qualification of Medical Practitioner. (b) Name of Applicant. (c) Period.	I (a).. hereby certify that (b) .... has been under my medical treatment for (c).......................... and that I deem it absolutely necessary and indispensible for the recovery of his health that he should have leave for a period of
	.... for the purpose of...
(d) Signature of Medical Practitioner. (e) Date of Certificate.	(d)...................................., (e).....................................,....,

IV.—Discipline.

A.—Offences Amenable to Discipline.

21. It shall be the duty of the Head of any of the various Offices to report to the Head of his Department all cases coming under his cognizance in which any official may appear to have been guilty of any of the following offences :—

(a) Absence from office during the prescribed office hours without leave or valid excuse.

(b) Performance of the duties of his office in a negligent or careless manner, or the neglect or omission to perform known duties, or refusal to obey the lawful instructions of his superior officer ; discourteous behaviour towards his superior or brother officers, or to those with whom he has to transact public business.

(c) Being under the influence of intoxicating beverages, especially during office hours.

(d) Pecuniary embarrassment, if occasioned by imprudence or other reprehensible cause.

(e) Having a decree for civil imprisonment issued against him.

(f) Becoming a party, under whatever plea, to accommodation bills, whether for his own purposes or for another person, and whether resulting in pecuniary embarrassment or not.

(g) Entering into a composition with creditors, or assigning his estate in any form, unless he can show that his difficulties have been occasioned by unavoidable misfortune, and not by extravagance or improvidence.

(h) Engaging for profit, either in or out of office hours, in any business or occupation other than his official duty, without the special consent of the Administrator.

No official is permitted to be a Director, or to engage either directly or indirectly in the management or direction of any public company or syndicate.

(i) Undertaking any private agency in any matter connected with the exercise or performance of his public duties.

(j) Becoming editor of a newspaper or taking any part in the management thereof, speaking in public or writing for newspapers, or other publications on political subjects ; writing anonymous letters, paragraphs, or articles in any public print, of any other than of a purely scientific or literary character.

(k) Giving any official information out of the strict course of duty, without the express permission or direction of the Head of the Department.

(l) Refusing or neglecting to give categorical answers to any questions put to him by, or by direction of, the Head of the Department, as to whether or not he has committed any of the offences mentioned in sub-sections (h), (i), (j) and (k) hereof.

(m) Being guilty of any conduct, or addicted to any habits which in the opinion of the Head of the Department are unbecoming a Civil Servant or inconsistent with the discharge of his duties.

(n) Habitually using intoxicating beverages to excess.

(o) Being convicted of any crime, and sentenced to imprisonment without the option of a fine, or becoming insolvent, in either of which cases he shall be deemed to have forfeited his office, and shall thereupon cease to perform his duties or receive his salary.

B.—*Procedure in Cases of Discipline.*

22. The offence with which such person is charged, with the grounds on which it rests, must be communicated in writing by the Head of the Office to the person against whom the information is laid, and such person shall be required to answer the charge in writing, within such period as may be specified in the notice conveyed to him.

23. Such answer, with any supporting evidence, shall be submitted without delay, to the Head of the Department ; who on receipt thereof, shall order such further enquiry as may seem to him desirable, or if no answer shall have been forwarded within such reasonable time as may have been allowed for that purpose, he shall submit the matter to the Administrator with his report thereon.

24. In case it may appear to the Head of the Office to be prejudicial to the interests of the Service to leave a person to whom an Offence is imputed, in the execution of his functions, he may at once, as a provisional measure, interdict such person from the further exercise of his functions, and from drawing his salary, pending the result of an immediate reference to the Head of the Department.

25. The Administrator may either acquit the accused of the charge preferred against him, or, upon the charge being sustained, may award such of the undermentioned punishments as the merits of the case may seem to require :—

(1) A reprimand.
(2) A fine.
(3) Suspension for a period, with or without deprivation of salary or emoluments.
(4) Reduction of salary or emoluments.
(5) Reduction in rank.
(6) Enforced resignation.
(7) Dismissal.

26. No person against whom any charge has been made shall be entitled to absent himself from the Territory pending the decision of his case without the special permission of the Head of the Department.

27. The Head of the Department may initiate proceedings against any person in his Department for any breach of discipline, although no charge in writing shall have been lodged with him.

SUPERANNUATION AND COMPENSATION ALLOWANCES.

28. From the salary of every person to whom a pension or gratuity may be assigned, there shall be made a monthly deduction at the rate of £3 per centum per annum on such salary ; provided that in no case shall any contribution be paid upon emoluments in excess of £1,200 per annum.

29. All officers who may be received on the fixed establishment and who may be in the Company's service in a civil capacity on the 1st April, 1898, will be allowed to elect whether they will commence their contributions from the 1st of April, 1898, or from a date not earlier than the date of their entering the Company's Civil employ ; and in the latter case they will be allowed to pay up the arrear percentage on half their salary, and for the purposes of pension or other compensation allowance the term of their service shall be in all cases calculated from the date from which they elect to pay the contribution aforesaid.

29(a). Every person who may be appointed on probation to any office mentioned in the Schedule A to these Regulations, may, within one month from the date of his appointment, elect whether or not he shall become a contributor to the Civil Service Pension Fund; and should he elect to become a contributor to such Fund, his contribution shall accrue from the date of his appointment.

In the event of his failing subsequently to qualify for appointment on the Fixed Establishment, the total amount of his contributions to the fund shall be refunded to him.

30. Officers placed on the fixed establishment shall not be entitled to retire on pension unless they are over 60 years of age, or are disabled by permanent infirmity of body or mind, or unless their offices are abolished, provided that in the case of telegraphists 50 should be read for 60.

31. An officer placed on pension while under 60 years of age, or 50 years in the case of telegraphists, being in a competent state of health, is liable to be called upon to accept suitable re-employment carrying equal rank and emoluments to those of his latest appointment, on penalty of forfeiture of his pension until he shall reach the age of 60, or in the case of telegraphists, 50. Provided that no such person shall be liable to be called upon to serve again if he shall have remained unemployed in service for a period of five years.

32. The following services do not count for pension :—

(1) Service rendered by any person while under 17 years of age.
(2) Service rendered by a contributor to the Civil Service Pension Fund in respect of which he may not have contributed to the Fund.
(3) Service rendered by any person appointed on probation unless he shall have elected to contribute during such period of probation.

33. No pension or gratuity may be granted :—

(1) To a person who, not being of a sufficient age or disabled, voluntarily retires from the Service, but in such cases the Company will refund to the officer retiring an amount equal to one-third of his contributions to the Fund.
(2) To any person remunerated solely by fees and allowances, or, with certain exceptions to be sanctioned by the Administrator, whose whole time in not given to the public service.
(3) To any person engaged in the discharge of duties of a purely temporary character.
(4) To any person who has not been a contributor to the Civil Service Pension Fund.
(5) To any person dismissed for misconduct.
(6) To any person engaged for a fixed term of months or years.

34. Any period of absence on leave may usually be counted as service for pension purposes, excepting any period of absence without salary. Provided that in case an officer is on leave of absence at the date of retirement he shall not, except in cases of leave on account of serious indisposition, be entitled to count more than two months of such leave as service for pension purposes.

35 Subject to these conditions and limitations a gratuity not exceeding one month's pay for each year of service may be granted to any person of less than ten years continuous service if his services are dispensed with, or, if being placed on the fixed establishment of the Civil Service, he is compelled to leave the service from infirmity of mind or body, or is found unfit to discharge the duties of his office.

36. If the holder of an office in respect of which a pension or gratuity may be granted is compelled to quit the service before the completion of ten years' continuous service, through some bodily injury occasioned without his own default in the discharge of his public duty, a gratuity of three months' pay for each year of service or a pension not exceeding one-sixth of his annual salary and emoluments may be granted to him, together with a free passage to Capetown or any such other railway station in South Africa as he may desire, and if, irrespective of the length of his service, his death results from such bodily injury, a gratuity not exceeding one month's pay for each year of service may be granted to his widow or minor children, or his parents, if depending on him for maintenance; or if such gratuity shall appear to the Administrator to be inadequate to meet the circumstances of the case, he may grant such sum, not exceeding a year's pay, as he may consider reasonable.

37. In the case of continuous service of ten years and upwards a pension of one-sixtieth of the average salary and emoluments upon which contribution to the Pension Fund shall have been paid may be granted to anyone entitled or required to retire on pension for every year's service which may lawfully be counted, not exceeding forty in any one case.

38. It shall be lawful for the Administrator to grant to any person retiring or removed from the fixed establishment of the Civil Service in consequence of the abolition of his office such special annual allowance, not exceeding two-thirds of the average salary and emoluments upon which contribution to the Pension Fund shall have been paid, by way of compensation as, on a full consideration of the circumstances of the case may seem to the said Administrator to be a reasonable and just compensation for the loss of office: Provided that such special annual allowance shall not exceed the amount which might be granted as pension if one third of the period of service which would have been counted for pension purposes were added thereto: Provided always that the number of years to be added shall in no case exceed such number as would, if added to the actual age of the person retiring or removed, make up sixty-five.

39. Should any person on the fixed establishment of the Civil Service be found to be unfit from any physical or other cause to discharge efficiently the duties of the particular office filled by him, or should it be found necessary to remove any person in order to facilitate improvements in the organisation of the Department to which any person belongs by which greater efficiency and economy can be effected, it shall be lawful for the Administrator, if such person shall have ten years' service or upwards, to place him on temporary pension pending the occurrence of a suitable vacancy, or if he shall have had less than ten years' service to dispense with his services on payment of a gratuity not

exceeding one month's pay for each year of service, precisely as if, in either case, he was not on the fixed establishment.

40. Service in respect of which superannuation or compensation allowances may be granted must in all cases be continuous, unless interrupted by reduction of office, leave of absence, or other temporary suspension of civil employment, not arising from any misconduct or voluntary resignation.

41. It shall be lawful for the Administrator to grant to a person to whom at his retirement any pension or gratuity may lawfully be granted, a superannuation, compensation, gratuity or other allowance, of greater amount than the amount which might be awarded to him under the foregoing provisions, when special services rendered by such person, and requiring special reward, shall appear to him to justify such increase, but so that such allowance shall in no case exceed the average salary and emoluments upon which contribution to the Pension Fund is being paid by such person at the time of his retirement ; and it shall be lawful for the Administrator to grant to any person any such allowance of less amount than otherwise would have been awarded to him, when his defaults or demerits in relation to the public service appear to him to justify such diminution.

42. After a superannuation or compensation allowance has been awarded to any person, the same may thereafter be rescinded in case it shall be discovered that during his tenure of office he was guilty of any offence which if known might have merited his dismissal, or if he shall refuse or neglect to comply with a reasonable request by the Administrator to perform some special duty in relation to the affairs of his late office.

43. The term "average salaries and emoluments" means the average of the preceding three years of salary (less local allowances), with fees, house rent, or house allowance, rations, and other remuneration for personal service added. But allowances for horse keep, travelling, etc., do not count for pension, nor may fees exceed one-fourth of the salary, or house allowance one-sixth of the salary and other emoluments, provided that in no case shall pension or other compensation allowances be calculated on emoluments, including allowances, in excess of £1,200 per annum

44. Nothing in the foregoing rules, Nos. 28 to 43 inclusive, shall preclude the Administrator from entering into such arrangements as may seem desirable with any Life Assurance Company or other Company or Association for the payment of annuities or other allowance to public officers in lieu of such pensions or other compensation allowances as are by the said rules provided for.

V.—Widow's Pension Fund.

45 Every officer who may be appointed to the fixed establishment subsequent to the 31st March, 1898, or who may elect to contribute during his period of probation, shall contribute to a Widow's Pension Fund at the rate of at least one per centum per annum on his salary and other emoluments counting for pension from the date on which he commences to contribute to the Civil Service Pension Fund, but he may increase such contribution if he wishes, and thereby secure to his widow a larger pension than she would be entitled to if he only contributed one per centum in the manner provided for in the Civil Service Acts and Regulations of the Cape Colony.

Should an officer who has contributed during his period of probation fail subsequently to qualify for appointment on the fixed establishment, the total amount of his contributions to the fund shall be refunded to him.

46. Every officer who may be on the fixed establishment on the 31st March, 1898, may elect to become a contributor to the Widow's Pension Fund, and, should he elect to contribute, his contributions shall commence from the 1st April, 1898.

47. The widows of all officers who have contributed to the Widow's Pension Fund shall be entitled to pensions calculated according to the tables of mortality in force in the Cape Colonial Civil Service, and subject to the Rules affecting the payment of such pensions in that Colony.

Regulations respecting Pensions which may be granted on their retirement to Officers who have served partly in the Civil Service of Rhodesia and partly in the Imperial or other Civil Service.†

48. These Regulations shall apply to all appointments made on and after the 1st day of January, 1897.

49. In these Regulations the words "other Government" or "other Civil Service" shall be taken to mean the Government or Civil Service, as the case may be, of any British Colony, or of any State, Territory or Civilised Power in South Africa, or of any Harbour Board in the Colonies of the Cape and Natal.

50. Whensoever in the case of any officer who has been taken from the Imperial or other service into that of the Company, the Administrator may grant him at his ultimate retirement any pension under the provisions of the "Civil Service Regulations," it shall be lawful to calculate such pension upon the whole period of his continuous service under the Imperial or other Government and that of the Company : Provided that the Imperial or other Government is prepared to contribute to the pension thus calculated an amount based on his period of service under the said Government, under any rules which may be in force at the time in the United Kingdom, or rules similar thereto.

51. Should the Imperial or other Government not be prepared to contribute as aforesaid, but on a period shorter than the whole period of the officer's service under that Government, such shorter period shall in that case be taken to be for pension purposes the officer's whole time under that Government.

52. Should the Imperial or other Government not be prepared to make any contribution to the pension of an officer taken as aforesaid into the service of the Company, any pension or gratuity which may lawfully be awarded to such officer shall be based solely on his period of service under the Company.

53. Should the period of service under the Company of any such officer to whose pension the Imperial or other Government is prepared to contribute

† The rules at present in force are given in Lord Granville's Circular Despatch, dated 15th July, 1869, and are affected by Lord Knutsford's Circular Despatch, dated 20th August, 1889. The rules in force in the Cape Colony are contained in G.N. 73 of 27th January, 1896.

be less than ten years, his retiring pension shall be calculated on his average salary and emoluments for the preceding ten years partly under the Imperial or other Government and partly under the Company.

Note.—Lord Knutsford in his Circular Despatch of the 20th August, 1889, states "that it has been decided that the Superannuation Act of 1859 does not allow of a pension being granted thereunder, in any circumstances whatever, to an officer of the Civil Service retiring from public employment under the age of 60 years, except on the ground of ill-health or abolition of office."

54. Whensoever in the case of an officer who has been taken, without a break, from the service of the Company into the Imperial or other service, the Imperial or other Government is prepared to grant him on his retirement, under such rules as may in that respect be in force at the time in the United Kingdom, or rules similar thereto, a pension based on his period of service under both Governments capable of being counted for pension purposes, the Administrator may sanction a contribution from the revenues of the Company towards such pension, for each year of his continuous service in this territory at the rate of one-sixtieth of his average salary and emoluments capable of being counted for pension purposes at the date when he is so taken over : Provided that no fractional part of a month may be taken into consideration : Provided further, that such officer retires from the Imperial or other service on grounds which would render it lawful for the Administrator to grant him a pension if he were then in the Civil Service of the Company.

55. Should an officer who had been taken from the Imperial or other service into the service of the Company be again taken without a break into the Imperial or other service, the Administrator, on the ultimate retirement of such officer on grounds on which he might lawfully retire on pension from the Civil Service of the Company, may sanction a contribution to his pension from the public revenue of an amount based on the period of his continuous service in this territory, his preceding service under the Imperial or other Government being taken into computation in accordance, *mutatis mutandis*, with regulations 2—5 hereof.

VI.—Security and Public Service Guarantee Fund.

56. It shall be the duty of the Administrator to fix and determine the amount of security to be given by the holder of any office in the Civil Service of the territory involving the receipt, custody, or payment of public money or the receipt, issue, or custody of stamps, and to frame a schedule for the guidance of public officers, showing the amount so fixed in respect of such offices, and from time to time to amend such schedule as circumstances may require.

57. The holders of offices from whom security is required shall be required to contribute to a fund styled the "Public Service Guarantee Fund," and all contributions or other moneys payable to the said fund shall be lodged to the credit of a separate deposit account.

58. From and after the 1st day of April, 1898, in any case where an officer who has not previously contributed to the Public Service Guarantee Fund holds, or is appointed to, any office in the public service of the Territory, the holder of which is required to give security, a deduction of one-eighth per cent. on the amount for which he is required to give security shall be made on account

of such fund from the first payment of salary in respect of such office, and such person shall further contribute to such fund at the rate of one-eighth per cent. per annum on such amount from the date of his entering on the discharge of the duties of such office.

59. Should any person appointed to any office in respect of which security is required have contributed to such fund in respect of an office previously held by him, he shall contribute to such fund at the rate of one-eighth per cent. per annum on the amount of security required in respect of such new office, and such contribution shall accrue from the date of his entering on the discharge of the duties of such new office, and the increase, if any, in the amount to be contributed shall for the first contribution be deducted from the first payment of salary in respect of such new office. Provided that if the period for which he shall have previously contributed shall not have expired, a portion of such previous contribution, proportionate to such unexpired period, shall be deducted from the first contribution required by this section.

60. Every person who may at any time hold an office in the public service of the territory in respect of which, in the opinion of the Administrator security should be given, but who has not been required to give any security, shall from a date appointed by the Administrator contribute to the Public Service Guarantee Fund as if he had been first appointed to such office at such date.

61. In respect of every first annual contribution to the said Fund, an amount proportionate to the period between the date from which it commences to accrue and the 31st of March next ensuing shall be deducted from the first payment of salary payable to the holder of the office in respect of which security is given, and thereafter the annual contribution shall be payable in advance on the 31st of March in each year, and shall be deducted from the payment of salary for the said month of March, and should any deduction not be made as prescribed herein, the amount shall be forthwith recovered from the person in default.

62. Should any person who has become a contributor to Public Service Guarantee Fund cause any pecuniary loss to the public revenue of the territory by reason of any wrongful act or omission, the amount of such loss shall be charged against such person and shall, as far as possible, be recovered in such manner as the Public Prosecutor may direct, and in case the amount recovered shall be insufficient to cover such loss, it shall be lawful for the Chief Accountant, on being authorised to do so by the Administrator, to pay out of the aforesaid fund such sum as shall be sufficient to make good the amount of loss sustained by the revenue, not exceeding, however, the amount for which security was given by the defaulter. Provided that if any amount be subsequently recovered from such defaulter, such amount shall be applied, firstly, to make good the deficiency (if any) still remaining due to the revenue and, secondly, to the re-imbursement of such fund.

Part IX.

SERVICES OF OFFICERS.

[Officers who have passed the Civil Service Law Examination are distinguished by an L].

ADCOCK, William Henry.—Appointed clerk, administrator's office, Bulawayo, July 6th, 1897 ; transferred to civil commissioner's office, Bulawayo, 1st July, 1901.

ADE, Edwin George.—Telegraphist, London, 25th April, 1892 ; to Cape service February, 1896 ; transferred to Rhodesian service as telegraphist 14th November, 1896 ; acting chief telegraphist, Salisbury, 1st July, 1900.

ASHMEAD, Herbert. — Assistant surveyor to the commissioners of Her Majesty's works and public buildings, 1st January, 1887 : chief inspector of public works, Rhodesia, 6th January, 1900, and accounting officer, mines and works, 1st June, 1900.

ATHERSTONE, William John.—Surveying in the Transvaal, 1892-1894 ; surveying in Cape Colony, 1895 : joined surveyor general's office, Rhodesia, July, 1898, as surveyor to B.S.A. Company ; assistant examiner, surveyor general's office, 1st May, 1901.

BAKER, Alfred Lee. Served in M.M. Police from 14th May, 1895, to 19th September, 1896 ; clerk chief accountant's office, 19th September, 1896 ; transferred on 22nd November, 1898, to civil commissioner's office, Umtali ; chief clerk, 2nd April, 1900.

BALCH, Horace Ethelbert.—Postal assistant, England, June, 1894 ; appointed to Rhodesian service as assistant, 23rd June, 1898 ; acting postmaster, Victoria, 13th July, 1900 ; postmaster, Melsetter, 1st June, 1901.

BARNARD, Mostyn William (L).—B.S.A.C.P., 1890-1, Mashonaland ; Mashonaland Mounted Police, 1893 ; served in Matabele War, 1893, in "A" troop Salisbury Horse, severely wounded Bembesi fight, 4th November, 1893 ; with Major Forbes at Tanganyika ; served in Matabele rebellion, 1896, in Grey's scouts (medal and clasp) ; sent on expedition to Karri Karri salt pans ; clerk to registrar, high court, Southern Rhodesia, 1st June, 1898 ; appointed assistant native commissioner, Matabeleland, 1st July, 1899.

BARNES, Francis Richard.—Postal assistant, England, Nov. 1892 ; transferred to Cape service (Capetown) 25th January, 1896 ; to Rhodesian service, as audit clerk at Salisbury, 17th March, 1897 ; postmaster, Kopje, 21st October, 1897 ; clerk, head office, Salisbury, 1st May, 1898.

BARRIE, Ninian.—Postmaster and telegraphist at Lobatsi, 15th July, 1896 ; assistant at Bulawayo, 1st September, 1898.

58 SERVICES OF OFFICERS.

BAXTER, ERNEST CHARLES.—Appointed accountant, distributor of stamps, J.P., R.M. clerk, taxing master, and chief clerk to postmaster general, Vryburg, British Bechuanaland, 1st October, 1885; assistant resident magistrate, 1st March, 1888; postmaster-general for Bechuanaland and Protectorate, July 1st, 1888, examiner of accounts on high commissioner's staff, Capetown, Feb. 8th, 1889, collector of customs for British Bechuanaland Jan., 1891; also for Bechuanaland Protectorate, July 1, 1893. In May, 1892, received the thanks of the secretary of state for the colonies for services rendered; owing to annexation of territory retired on pension 15th Feb., 1896; collector of customs, Southern Rhodesia, 1st July, 1899; J.P. for Southern Rhodesia.

BAYLEY, CECIL.—Joined B.S.A. police, November, 1890; was transferred to administrator's office, 1st November, 1893; secretary law department, 1st March, 1895; sheriff of Rhodesia, 28th April, 1897; acted as magistrate, Salisbury, 23rd August, 1897, to end of 1898, and at Umtali, 16th March to 10th June, 1899; is J.P. for Southern, Rhodesia.

BAYNE, LOUIS LOCHEE (L).—Appointed clerk on probation, Cape Government Railways, 1st February, 1893; clerk customs, Port Elizabeth, 23rd May, 1893; assistant examining officer, Capetown, 10th July, 1896; examining officer, Capetown, 31st December, 1896; inspector of bonded warehouses, 30th November, 1898; transferred to Southern Rhodesia Customs as examining officer, Umtali, 11th July, 1899; Salisbury, 24th May, 1900; sub-collector Salisbury, 1st April, 1901.

BEADLE, ARTHUR WILLIAM.—Clerk, Cape Government Railways, November, 1897; clerk, accounts department, Cape office, 1st April, 1899.

BEATY-POWNALL, EDWARD GEORGE.—Clerk, mines department, 19th Oct.,

1896; assistant claim inspector and clerk, 1st April, 1897.

BELL, ADAM.—Extra A.D.C. to Governor and Commander-in-Chief, Capetown, 1879-80; representative B.S.A. Co., Mafeking, Palapye, Francistown and Matoppos, 1st August, 1896, to 6th December, 1897; receiving and delivery agent for B.S.A. Co., Bulawayo, 7th December, 1897, sub-collector of customs, Bulawayo, 1st August, 1899; J.P. for Matabeleland.

BELL, ADAM BORRADAILE.—Clerk chief accountant's department, 4th August, 1899; detached for special duty as officer in charge of the Range Depôt, Rhodesia Field Force, April, 1900.

BERRY, THOMAS.—Appointed accountant at Kimberley, May, 1890; accountant, Capetown, July, 1895; chief accountant, Bulawayo, July, 1896; chief accountant, Salisbury, January, 1897.

BIDDULPH, WILLIAM THOMAS.—Served through the Matabele war, 1896 (medal); clerk, master's department, Bulawayo, August, 1896; transferred to master's office, Salisbury, November, 1896; detached for duty in administrator's office, January, 1897; resumed duty, master's office, July, 1897; appointed acting chief clerk to master and assistant registrar, April, 1899.

BIRCH, CULLUM DE KANTZOU.—Joined Cape mounted rifles, January, 1890; lieutenant Bulawayo field force, rebellion, 1896; lieutenant Legion des Philhéllénes, Turko-Greek war, 1897; lieutenant 1st regiment cavalry, Greek army, October, 1897; appointed cattle inspector, Salisbury district, 1st February, 1899.

BIRCH, JOHN DE GRAY.—Joined the B.S.A. Co. forces 3rd April, 1896; appointed lieutenant, November, 1896; sub-inspector, municipal police of Mashonaland, 1st March, 1897; justice of the peace for province of Mashonaland, July, 1897; acted as officer commanding Mashonaland municipal police, July-December, 1897; acting inspector of locations, Umtali, November, 1898; inspector, Mashonaland constabulary, 1st January, 1901.

BLACKWELL, JOHN SIDNEY.—Clerk to civil commissioner, Salisbury, January 1, 1900; clerk to inspector of schools and statist, April 1, 1900.

BLANCKENBERG, CHARLES HENRY.—Joined M.M. police, 1895; appointed clerk, Capetown office, March, 1896; transferred to administrator's office, Bulawayo, March, 1897; resigned June, 1897; rejoined B.S.A. Co. Capetown office, April, 1898; tranferred to administrator's office, Bulawayo, March, 1899; transferred to the surveyor-general's office, Salisbury, 1st November, 1901.

BLANCKENBERG, REGINALD ANDREW (L). — Appointed clerk to B.S.A. Co.'s Capetown office, February, 1895; transferred to Mafeking, April, 1896; transferred to administrator's office, Bulawayo, September, 1896; appointed private secretary to administrator of Matabeleland, April, 1899; lent to surveyor-general's office, August, 1901.

BLANCKENBERG, WILLIAM ROSSEAU (L).—Appointed magistrate's office, Bulawayo, 14th July, 1899.

BOARDMAN, CLEMENT HAMILTON CRAUSE.—Joined Rhodesian telegraphs, October, 1892; chief accountant's office as examiner of accounts, March, 1898; relieving clerk, civil commissioner's office, Salisbury, 17th December, 1900, to 7th May, 1901.

BOARDMAN, JAMES.—Postal assistant, Cape Colony, January 16th, 1897; to Rhodesian service as postal assistant at Salisbury, October 1st, 1897; to Selukwe as postmaster, September 1st, 1900.

BOWEN, GEORGE JOHN.—Claim inspector, May, 1893; mining commissioner, March, 1894.

BRAILSFORD, EDWARD ARTHUR LAW (L).—Served as a volunteer during the Gcaleka war and Gaika rebellion, 1877-78 (medal with clasp); temporary clerk to the resident magistrate, Tarka, August, 1880; second clerk to the civil commissioner and resident magistrate at Somerset East, July, 1882; assistant resident magistrate, May, 1883; acting senior clerk and distributor of stamps, Victoria West, July, 1886; has acted on several occasions as civil commissioner and resident magistrate at Somerset East, Victoria West, and Bedford, and at Herbert from October, 1896 to October, 1898; chairman of the rinderpest committee during the above period, and as such rendered special services; chairman of the advisory board appointed to advise the government in connection with the Douglas irrigation works, 1897; rendered special services in connection with the Campbell water servitude dispute, 1898; transferred to the Southern Rhodesia civil service as magistrate of Salisbury, 1st November, 1898; acting magistrate, Bulawayo, 1st July, 1900.

BRERETON, HARDMAN JOHN KER.— Mashonaland constabulary (Mashonaland municipal police), 19th March, 1898; promoted sub-inspector and inspector of licences, 1st March, 1901.

BRIGGS, ALBERT EDWIN. — Appointed clerk, administrator's office, 12th September, 1897; inspector of licences for Mashonaland, 1st February, 1899; clerk, surveyor general's office, 1st November, 1901.

BRIGGS, CHARLES WILLIAM.—Overseer of works, Salisbury sanitary board and engineer to municipality, 1897; inspector of roads, 1st August, 1899.

BROOKS, JOHN ABBOTT. — Cape postal and telegraph department, May, 1894; to Rhodesian service, as assistant, 11th August, 1898.

BROUN, FREDERICK STUART. — Magistrate, N.W.T., Canada, 1892-

1895 : Matabeleland mounted police, 1895-1897 ; claim inspector and clerk, mines department, 15th July, 1897.

BROWN, ALLEN HENRY.—Entered London office, B.S.A. Co., 9th November, 1896 ; confidential clerk to manager, 1st January, 1898 ; transferred to chief secretary's office, Salisbury, 22nd July, 1901.

BYERS, BASIL HAROLD.—Clerk to company's agent at Mafeking and at rail head, 15th July, 1896 ; to administrator's office, Bulawayo, 17th June, 1897 ; to assistant controller's department, 1st August, 1899.

BYRON, FREDERICK ROCHFORT.—Joined B.S.A. police, April, 1891 ; acting tax collector and fieldcornet Marandella district, November, 1894 ; clerk, master's office, Salisbury, February, 1895—October, 1897 ; ranger to Salisbury sanitary board, November, 1897 ; appointed acting native commissioner, M'toko, October, 1897.

CAMPBELL, ARCHIBALD ANDREW.—Superintendent of natives, Dundee, Natal, 1895 ; appointed native commissioner, Matabeleland, 1st November, 1896 ; justice of the peace, 1897 ; special J.P., 3rd February, 1899.

CAMPBELL, CHARLES MERCER.—Clerk, mines department, 15th September, 1895 ; assistant claim inspector, 1st July, 1896 ; claim inspector and clerk, 1st April, 1898.

CARBUTT, CLIVE LANCASTER.—Formerly in the Zululand civil service ; appointed assistant native commissioner, 6th February, 1897 ; acting native commissioner, 1st April, 1898 ; native commissioner, 1st June, 1899 ; justice of the peace, 1898.

CARSON, ERNEST HOPE.—Appointed to administrator's office, Salisbury, November, 1896 ; served in Matabeleland and Mashonaland rebellions, 1896-7 (medal and clasp) ; on active service in Natal and Transvaal from November, 1899.

CARY, CHARLES WALKER.—Maintenance officer and telegraphist, Charter, 15th April, 1892 ; telegraphist, Salisbury, 11th July, 1895 ; civil commissioner's and magistrate's clerk, Tuli, 1st January, 1896 ; acting civil commissioner and company's representative, Tuli, 6th February, 1896 ; clerk, master's office, Bulawayo, 10th April ; chief clerk, 1st June, 1897 ; transferred magistrate's office, as clerk of the civil court, 1st December, 1897.

CASTENS, HERBERT HAYTON.—B.A. ; called to the bar at the Inner Temple, May, 1889 ; and admitted to the bar of the supreme court (Capetown), March, 1890 ; appointed acting public prosecutor, Southern Rhodesia, May, 1897 ; chief secretary, 20th June, 1899.

CHATAWAY, NORMAN HARRIS.—M.M. police, 1895 ; served in Matabele rebellion, 1896 ; appointed clerk, chief accountant's office of B S.A. Company, Bulawayo, March, 1896 ; transferred to Salisbury, January, 1897 ; to accountant's office, Bulawayo, May, 1898 ; acting accountant, May, 1901 ; secretary, tender board, Matabeleland, January, 1899, to October, 1901.

CLOETE, HENRY ARTHUR.—Clerk-in-charge B.S.A. Company's telegraph audit department, Capetown, 1891 ; chief clerk to civil commissioner and magistrate, Umtali, April, 1897 ; has acted as civil commissioner and magistrate, Umtali, on several occasions ; acting civil commissioner and magistrate, Melsetter, 15th November, 1898 ; on special duty buying cattle in Australia, 1900 ; acting native commissioner, Umtali, February to June, 1901 ; secretary and accountant, customs department, 21st July, 1901.

CLOETE, SEBASTIAN VALENTINE.—Clerk, Capetown office of B.S.A. Company, April, 1891 ; was auditor in North - Eastern Rhodesia for seven months during 1894 ; returned to Capetown, October, 1894 ; transferred to chief accountant's office, Bulawayo,

December, 1896 ; to Salisbury, Feb., 1897 ; accountant, Bulawayo, May, 1898.

COLEMAN, JOSEPH WILLIAM.— Postal assistant, England, 18th February, 1891 ; transferred to Cape service, 21st December, 1895 ; to Rhodesian service as telegraphist, 10th December 1896 ; clerk, head office, 8th July, 1898.

COLLYER, JOHN.—Telegraph department, England, 28th September, 1891 ; transferred to Cape service, 2nd November, 1895 ; joined Rhodesia service as telegraphist, 10th February, 1897 ; chief telegraphist, Salisbury, 1st February, 1900 ; acting superintendent telegraph office, Bulawayo, 12th August, 1901.

COOKE, CONRAD BERNARD.— Served through the Langalebalea rebellion, 1873-74 ; admitted as Zulu interpreter to resident magistrate courts, Natal, 26th June, 1879 ; served as native levy leader in the Zulu war (medal, 1879) ; admitted as an attorney of the supreme court of the Colony of Natal, January, 1885 ; appointed sub-inspector of the Matabeleland native police, 1st December, 1895 ; served in the Matabeleland rebellion, 1896 (medal) ; appointed acting assistant native commissioner and registrar of natives, 1st April, 1896 ; native commissioner, 1st September, 1896 ; acting native commissioner, Mzingwani district, June, 1897 ; justice of the peace, 21st September, 1897 ; acting native commissioner for Bulilima-Mangwe district, 8th May, 1899.

COOPE, JOHN CHARLES JESSER.— Inspector of roads, January, 1892 ; paymaster under vote IV./3, Matabeleland, 8th May, 1900.

CORDNER, HENRY.—Assistant postmaster, Salisbury, 1st August, 1894 ; transferred as clerk, general stores department, December, 1894 ; manager of general stores, February, 1897 ; transferred to chief accountant's office ; December, 1897 ; transferred as super-

intendent, stationery department, 1st March, 1899.

CRAGO, THOMAS. — Telegraphist, Great Britain, May, 1885, to November, 1892 : Telegraphist, West Australia, October, 1896 to November, 1898 ; telegraphist, Cape Colony, January, 1899 to August, 1899 ; telegraphist, Rhodesia, 1st September, 1899.

CRAKE, EDRED AUGUSTINE.—Appointed clerk to sub-collector of customs, Bulawayo, 1st July, 1899 ; served with S.R.V. under Col. Plumer, November, 1899 to July, 1900 ; clerk and assistant warehouse-keeper, Bulawayo, 16th April, 1901.

CRAVEN, PERCIVAL EDWARD. — Joined the service of the B.S.A. Co., October, 1890 ; appointed clerk in the secretary's department, 28th November, 1890 ; clerk in mines office, February, 1891 ; postmaster, Salisbury, April, 1891 ; clerk in accountant's department, June, 1891 ; acting accountant from 7th September, 1893, to 31st January, 1894 ; accountant and principal distributor of stamps from 1st February, 1894, to 31st March, 1897 ; accountant to chief secretary and principal distributor of stamps from 1st April, 1897.

CREWE, CECIL.—B.A. Oxon ; clerk to magistrate, Salisbury, 20th June, 1900.

DE SMIDT, JOHN PASCOE LARKINS (L). — Clerk, Cape customs, 2nd January, 1890 ; appointed inspector of customs and resident magistrate's clerk, Simonstown, October, 1894 ; assistant resident magistrate, Uniondale, December, 1895 ; assistant resident magistrate, Tulbagh, July, 1896 ; acting chief clerk, resident magistrate's office, Capetown, March, 1897 ; assistant resident magistrate and chief clerk, Clanwilliam, March, 1897 : transferred to Rhodesian civil service as assistant magistrate, Victoria, 27th November, 1897 ; acted as civil commissioner and magistrate from May to November, 1898 ; appointed civil commissioner and magistrate, Tuli, 9th January, 1899.

DE STADLER, PETRUS JACOBUS.— Cape postal department, August, 1888 ; to Rhodesian service as assistant, October, 1895 ; postmaster, March, 1896.

DEVINE, WILLIAM ALFRED.— Entered Rhodesia telegraph department, 1st October, 1897 ; clerk, telegraph audit, 26th September, 1898 ; clerk, secretarial branch, G.P.O., 30th November, 1898.

DOBSON, JOHN. — Telegraphist, United Kingdom, from 20th June, 1888, to 5th May, 1891 ; telegraphist, Persia (under Indian government), 11th May, 1891, to 11th May, 1894 ; telegraphist, West Australia, 2nd October, 1896, to 15th March, 1900 ; telegraphist, Rhodesia, 21st March, 1900.

DOUGLAS, JOHN CHARLES EDWARD. —B.A., Oxon, barrister-at-law ; clerk, mines department, 8th February, 1901.

DOWNING, ALBERT WILLIAM.— Victorian postal and telegraph department, 20th December, 1892 ; entered Rhodesia postal and telegraph department 11th April, 1900.

DUFF, COLIN ERIC.—Joined Capetown office, November, 1894 ; transferred to chief accountant's office, Salisbury, February, 1898 ; transferred to chief secretary's office, September, 1898 ; clerk, Capetown office, April, 1901.

DUNBAR, STONEWELL TEMPLE.— Appointed clerk in general stores department, 18th May, 1896 ; clerk in charge stationery department, December, 1897 ; transferred to chief accountant's office as examiner of accounts, 1st March, 1899.

DUTHIE, GEORGE.—M.A. (Aber.), B.A. (Cantab.), F.R.S.E., superintending inspector of schools and statist, 1901.

DUTTON, PIERS EDWIN.—Clerk in controller's office, Salisbury, November 17th, 1898 ; acting accountant for controller's department, February 24th, 1901 ; acting in charge of stores department, Salisbury, July 1st, 1901.

DREW, ALFRED. — Joined B.S.A. police, September, 1890 ; clerk to resident magistrate, Victoria, 1st October, 1892 ; native commissioner, Victoria, 1st September, 1894 ; served in Matabele war, 1896, and as lieutenant in charge native contingent, Mashona rebellion, 1896-7.

EARL, HENRY EDWARD.—Postal and telegraph department of United Kingdom, June, 1897 to April, 1900 ; telegraphist, Rhodesia, 14th April, 1900.

EDDIE, NORMAN LINDSAY KAYE.— Messenger of court and locker of customs, Gwelo, and issuer of process, Selukwe, 6th January, 1900 ; clerk, surveyor general's office, 1st November, 1900.

EDWARDS, WILLIAM.—Native commissioner, M'Rewa and Marandella, 1st May, 1895 ; assistant native commissioner, M'Rewa, 1st April, 1897 ; native commissioner, 1st October, 1900.

EICKHOFF, CHARLES. — Telegraphist, London, 27th October, 1883 : resigned Imperial services, 18th May, 1896 ; joined Rhodesian service as telegraphist, 26th December, 1897 ; acting postmaster, Umtali, 8th August, 1900.

ELLIS, RICHARD. — Telegraphist, England, 5th September, 1892 ; entered Cape service as telegraphist, 28th September, 1895 ; entered Rhodesian service as assistant, 15th September, 1898.

ELLIOTT, FREDERICK GEORGE.— Formerly in Zululand civil service ; appointed native commissioner, Matabeleland, 1st November, 1897 : justice of the peace : inspector native compounds, 1st August, 1900.

ELLIOTT, HENRY ALBERT.—Formerly in Natal civil service ; clerk and interpreter, magistrate's court, Gwelo ; assistant native commissioner, Matabeleland, 27th July, 1899 ; justice of the peace.

EMERTON, ARTHUR FREDERICK.—
Clerk, accountant's office, G.P.O., Capetown, March, 1890; accountant, G.P.O.,
Salisbury, February, 1897 ; secretary,
G.P.O., Salisbury, 1st September, 1897;
member stamp commission and member tender board, November, 1900 ;
acting postmaster-general, 19th March,
1901 to 18th October, 1901.

EVERED, HAROLD ROBERT.—Postal
and telegraph department, United
Kingdom, 1896; telegraphist, Rhodesia,
21st April, 1899.

EYRE, GEORGE HENRY. — Telegraphist at Derby (England), 1876 ;
clerk, telegraph engineering branch,
Nottingham, October, 1880 ; to Cape
service as telegraphist at Capetown,
January, 1883 ; superintendent, circu-
lation branch, G.P.O., Capetown, October, 1885; principal clerk, foreign mails
branch, secretarial department, G.P.O.;
chief clerk, postmaster general's staff,
Capetown, 1st July, 1893 ; transferred
to Rhodesian service as postmaster-
general, 6th February, 1897 ; assistant
commissioner of mines and works,
Salisbury, 14th September, 1897 to
31st March, 1900.

FAIRBAIRN, KENNETH BRUCE.—
Assistant clerk of the papers, legislative
council, Capetown, June, 1894 ; joined
Rhodesia civil service, January, 1899 ;
additional assistant registrar, high
court also acts as clerk to Mr. Justice
Watermeyer.

FARMANER, GEORGE WILLIAM.—
Joined B.S.A. police, 26th November ;
1889 ; appointed clerk in survey department, 15th September, 1891 ;
appointed chief clerk, civil commissioner, Salisbury, 1st April, 1893 ;
appointed civil commissioner, Umtali,
1st June, 1894 ; appointed acting
magistrate, Umtali, 1st September,
1895 ; appointed assistant civil
commissioner and magistrate, Salisbury, 1st March, 1897; appointed
acting civil commissioner, Salisbury,
21st September, 1897 ; appointed civil

commissioner, Salisbury, 1st December,
1898.

FIELDE, WILLIAM RANDAL.—Joined
Capetown office, May, 1894 ; transferred to administrator's office, Salisbury, July, 1895 ; acting clerk to
council, July, 1895 to May, 1899 ;
assistant clerk to the legislative and
executive councils, 1st May, 1899 ;
clerk, chief secretary's office, March,
1900.

FISHER, FREDERICK.—Joined B.B.
police, 10th August, 1892 ; served
through Matabele campaign, 1893-4
(medal) ; accountant to collector of
customs, Southern Rhodesia, 9th July,
1899 ; acting sub-collector, Bulawayo,
8th May, 1901 ; officer-in-charge customs, Umtali, 1st August, 1901.

FISHER, JOHN THORNHILL (L).—
Appointed clerk to native commissioner,
Charter district, 22nd November,
1898 ; clerk in charge, Chilimanzi
native district, 18th December, 1899.

FLEMING, ANDREW MILROY, C.M.G.,
M.B., C.M. Edin. Univ., 1893. Late
assistant physician to Victoria hospital
for consumption and diseases of the
chest, Edinburgh, 1893 ; late junior
house surgeon, Carnarvon hospital,
Kimberley, 1894 ; medical officer in
charge Salisbury hospital, October,
1894 ; acted as principal medical
officer to B.S.A. Co.'s forces, Mashonaland, during 1896-97 rebellion ; appointed medical director and inspector
to the B.S.A. Co. and principal medical
officer, B.S.A. police, April, 1897 ; cr.
C.M.G. May, 1898.

FLEMING, CHARLES DAVID.—Clerk,
mines department, February, 1896 ;
acting mining commissioner, November, 1897 ; mining commissioner, 1st
April, 1899.

FLEMING, GEORGE NORVAL.—Clerk
to civil commissioner and statist, June,
1897 ; clerk, mines department, 23rd
February, 1898.

FLETCHER, CHARLES MCKENZIE.—
Cape civil service, December, 1890 ;

transferred colonial secretary's office, August, 1895 : joined Rhodesia civil service, 19th August, 1896, as magistrate's clerk, Bulawayo : acting assistant magistrate, October, 1898 ; acting chief clerk, public prosecutor's department, Bulawayo, April, 1899.

FORBES, PATRICK WILLIAM.—Appointed to command a troop in B.S.A.C. police, 16th November, 1889 ; represented B.S.A. Company in Manica in November, 1890 ; appointed magistrate, Hartley, 29th June, 1891 ; magistrate, Salisbury, 30th October, 1891 ; marriage officer, Salisbury and Hartley, 3rd March, 1892 ; magistrate, Victoria, 20th December, 1892 ; commanded company forces in first Matabele war, October, November and December, 1893 ; appointed magistrate, Bulawayo, 14th November, 1893 ; appointed administrator of Northern Rhodesia, 30th June, 1895 ; staff officer of volunteers, 24th October, 1898.

FORRESTALL, PETER. Joined B.S.A. police, January, 1890 ; served through Matabele war, 1893 ; native commissioner, Charter district, 1st October, 1894 ; native commissioner, Victoria District, January, 1896 ; native commissioner, Chibi district, December, 1896.

FOX, FRANK WILSON.—Appointed to administrator's office, Salisbury, September, 1896 ; served in Matabeleland and Mashonaland rebellions, 1896-7 (mentioned in despatches ; medal and clasp).

FREEMAN, DANIEL CHRISTOPHER.—Postal and telegraph department, South Australia, 1st June, 1888 ; telegraphist, Rhodesia, 11th April, 1900.

FULLER, JOHN WILLIAMS.— Joined Bechuanaland border police as trooper, 8th May, 1886 ; promoted sub-lieutenant, 29th December, 1887 ; lieutenant, 1st April, 1889 ; captain, 16th April, 1890 ; appointed magistrate of

N'Gamiland, and to command expedition of Bechuanaland border police, and Boer trekkers to lake N'Gami in February, 1895 ; transferred to Cape police as inspector, district No. 2 on annexation of British Bechuanaland to Cape Colony, 27th November, 1895 ; commanded force consisting of Cape police and Vryburg volunteers in Bechuana rebellion in January, 1897 ; appointed as intelligence officer on the staff of Colonel Dalgety commanding troops at the Langeberg in 1897 ; transferred to Mashonaland constabulary (Mashonaland municipal police) as chief inspector on 12th September, 1899.

FYNN, CHARLES GAWER. — Appointed native commissioner, Gwanda district, 19th October, 1895 ; registrar of natives, Bulawayo, 30th October, 1896 ; acting N.C., Belingwe, 3rd May, 1900 ; J.P., Matabeleland.

FYNN, HILTON CLIFFORD KNIGHT.— Joined Cape forest department, Ft. Cunynghame, 2nd April, 1892 ; forester in charge Kologha forests, June, 1892 ; clerk in conservator of forests' office, Kingwilliamstown, March 1893 ; assistant to conservator of forests, eastern conservancy, 1st June, 1893 ; served in Bechuanaland field force, Langeberg campaign, 1897 ; appointed clerk, chief native commissioner's office, Salisbury, 18th April, 1898 ; acting native commissioner, Marondella, 3rd April, 1901.

FYNN, MELVYN DICK. — Joined Cape mounted police 1st January, 1893, and served until June, 1899 ; served in the Bechuanaland field force, Langeberg campaign, 1897 ; appointed assistant native commissioner, South Mazoe, October, 1899 ; justice of the peace, South Mazoe district, June, 1900.

FYNN, PERCIVAL DONALD LESLIE (L).— Joined public works department, Kingwilliamstown, 15th November, 1889 ; transferred to office of secretary to the law department, Capetown, 23rd

August, 1893, thence to colonial secretary's office, November, 1894 ; chief examiner of accounts, colonial secretary's department, January, 1896 ; transferred to B.S.A. Company's service and appointed to native department, 1st January, 1897 ; transferred to chief accountant's office, as chief examiner of accounts, June, 1897; appointed auditor and inspector, April, 1898 ; acting chief accountant, August, 1900.

GILLESPIE, DAVID.—Chief clerk, G.P.O., Salisbury, 17th February, 1897 ; accountant, G.P.O. Salisbury, 1st September, 1897.

GILLILAND, GEORGE SAMUEL SLATER.—Postal and telegraph assistant, Edinburgh, July, 1891 ; entered Cape service as telegraphist, December, 1896 ; entered Rhodesian service as telegraphist, 21st April, 1898 ; clerk, G.P.O., Salisbury, 13th June, 1900.

GLANVILLE, THOMAS GENT.— G.P.O., London, September, 1890 ; transferred to Cape service, 16th May, 1896 ; entered Rhodesian service as assistant, 16th January, 1899.

GOLDSCHMIDT, HENRY TEMPLE.— Clerk, Capetown office, March, 1891 ; transferred to Salisbury, as secretary to council, May, 1895 ; transferred to Bulawayo as private secretary to Dr. Jameson, September, 1895 ; attached temporarily to Cape o'fce, January, 1896 ; transferred to Bulawayo, June, 1896 ; appointed acting secretary to administrator, Bulawayo, September, 1896 ; transferred to Salisbury, April, 1897 ; appointed acting secretary, Bulawayo ; March, 1898 ; appointed assistant secretary, Bulawayo, April, 1899 ; transferred to Cape office, June, 1899.

GORDON, FRANK JAMES. — Appointed sub-inspector Matabeleland native police, 1st December, 1895 ; assistant native commissioner, 1st September, 1896; acting native commissioner from 1st June, 1897, to 28th February, 1898 ; served in Matabele rebellion, 1896 (medal) ; appointed justice of the peace, 1897.

GOWERS, WILLIAM FREDERICK, B.A. —Appointed clerk native department, Matabeleland, 1st January, 1899 ; assistant native commissioner, 1st May, 1900.

GRANGER, CHARLES FREDERICK.— Acting clerk to magistrate, Bulawayo, August, 1896 ; clerk to H.H. Judge Watermeyer, 5th September, 1896, and additional assistant registrar : assistant registrar, 6th July, 1899.

GRAY, C. E., M.R.C.V.S.—Chief veterinary surgeon ; appointed postal telegraphs, Edinburgh, Scotland, 1879 ; volunteer, Nile Expedition, 1884-5 (medal, clasp and star); graduated Royal (Dick) Veterinary College, Edinburgh ; appointed Rhodesian telegraphs, January, 1896 ; acting government veterinary surgeon, March ; volunteer, Selous' troop, Matabele rebellion (medal) ; November, 1897, six months' special rinderpest duty for native department, Transkei ; subsequently returned to Salisbury as government veterinary surgeon : appointed chief veterinary surgeon, June, 1901.

GREER, HENRY FRANCIS.—Clerk and Zulu interpreter in Natal civil service ; appointed clerk to native department, Matabeleland, 1st August, 1899.

GRIFFIN, TOWNSHEND. — Mining commissioner, 10th October, 1894 ; commissioner of mines and public works, 1st October, 1897.

HANCOCK, WILLIAM PATRICK THOMAS. — Victorian postal and telegraph department, 1891 ; postal and telegraph assistant, Rhodesia, 11th April, 1900.

HARBORD, RALPH ASSHETON.— Appointed accountant to C.C. Bulawayo, April, 1895 ; acting accountant, Salisbury, March, 1896 ; chief accountant's office, March, 1897 ; accountant to controller, T & S., April, 1897 ; acting controller, T. & S., May, 1898 ;

assistant to chief accountant, October, 1898.

HARLEY, EDWIN CECIL. — Postal department Orange Free State, May, 1890 ; entered Rhodesian service, November, 1896 ; chief postal assistant, Bulawayo, 1st October, 1900.

HARPER, HARRY ADAM.— Six years in Cape civil service ; postmaster, January, 1894 ; chief clerk, public works department, 1st January, 1895 ; paymaster, mines and works, 8th June, 1899.

HARPER, RICHARD BIRT. — Appointed to forest department, eastern conservancy, Cape Colony, 8th June, 1895 ; resigned appointment on 16th January, 1899 ; appointed clerk to native commissioner of Belingwe, 13th February, 1899 ; transferred to civil commissioner's office, Bulawayo, 6th July, 1899.

HARRIS, GEORGE TEMPLE.—Clerk, administrator's office, Bulawayo, July, 1897 ; clerk, civil commissioner's office, Bulawayo, September, 1897.

HARRIS, THOMAS HENRY.—Telegraphist, United Kingdom, March, 1880 ; postal department, Cape Colony, January, 1882 ; Transvaal, April, 1887 ; telegraphist, Rhodesia, 1st September, 1899 ; postmaster, Palapye, 1st February, 1900.

HAWKSLEY, JOHN ARTHUR DOUGLAS.—Clerk, mines department, 1st October, 1895 ; claim inspector and clerk, 1st April, 1897 ; acting mining commissioner, 26th January, 1900.

HEARN, HARRY WILLIAM.—Joined the British South Africa Company's police, December, 1890 ; left on disbandment of force in 1891 ; joined Mashonaland mounted police, May, 1895 ; gaoler at Victoria, April, 1897 ; clerk to civil commissioner and magistrate, Victoria, November, 1897 ; served in Mashonaland rebellion, 1896-97.

HEYMAN, ARTHUR AUGUSTUS INGLIS.—Clerk, mines department, 1st July, 1898 ; acting mining commissioner, 1st

November, 1899 ; mining commissioner 1st August, 1900.

HISCOCK, WILLIAM JOHN.— Called to the Bar, Inner Temple, June, 1888 ; clerk, mines department, 17th July, 1899.

HOAL, EDGAR.—Transferred from Cape telegraph and postal service to B.S.A. Company's posts and telegraphs; appointed to Melsetter as magistrate's clerk, January, 1896.

HOLE, HUGH MARSHALL, B.A.— Clerk in Kimberley office of B.S.A. Company, April, 1890 ; transferred to Capetown, April, 1891 ; to Salisbury, Mashonaland, May, 1891 ; acting secretary to administrator, 1892 ; C.C., Salisbury, April, 1893 ; registrar of deeds for Mashonaland, 1893 ; acting magistrate of Salisbury, 1893 ; C.C. and magistrate, 1895 ; secretary to administrator of Matabeleland, December, 1898 ; is a J.P. for Southern Rhodesia ; served as lieutenant in Rhodesia Horse during Mashona rebellion, 1896 ; on special service, Aden, in connection with Arab labour, June, 1901 ; appointed civil commissioner and government representative, Bulawayo, 1st July, 1901.

HOLLAND, ARTHUR HERBERT.— Clerk, Kingwilliamstown, 11th February, 1892 ; Queenstown, 11th October, 1892 ; acting chief clerk, Cathcart, September, 1893 ; returned to Queenstown, September, 1893 ; treasury, 21st October, 1893 ; prime minister's office 1st May, 1895 ; transferred to Rhodesia civil service as clerk in administrator's office, 1st January, 1897 ; private secretary to his honour the senior administrator, 1st January, 1900.

HOLLAND, ALFRED THORNHILL.— Clerk in the accountant C. S. department, 11th January, 1898 ; served with the Mashonaland squadron, Rhodesia regiment, in the Transvaal war, February to November, 1900 (medal and clasps) ; transferred to the chief native commissioner's office in January, 1901.

HOLLOWAY, ALFRED ERNEST.—
Joined Rhodesian postal department,
1st April, 1893; chief clerk, G.P.O.,
Salisbury, 31st July, 1897.

HONE, PERCY FREDERICK.—B.A.,
Cambridge; clerk, mines department,
29th August, 1900.

HONEY, WILFRED HALSTED LOUIS.
—Joined B.S.A. police in 1891; served
as volunteer in Matabele war, 1893
(medal); appointed chief clerk to civil
commissioner, Bulawayo, 1st December,
1893; secretary to deputy administrator, Northern Rhodesia, May, 1895;
in command "Honey's scouts,"
Mashonaland rebellion, 1896 (clasp);
appointed civil commissioner and resident magistrate, Tuli, 1897; justice of
peace for Rhodesia; sub-collector of
customs, Umtali, 1st July, 1899; on
special service with Rhodesia field force,
16th February to 10th December,
1900, acting assistant controller, 11th
December, 1900; acting civil commissioner, Bulawayo, 17th April, 1901;
assistant civil commissioner, 1st July,
1901.

HOOK, DAVID WORTH. — Clerk
customs, Port Elizabeth, 1896; appointed clerk, chief native commissioner's office, Salisbury, 11th May,
1897; clerk in charge, Southern Mazoe,
1st October, 1898; chief native commissioner's office, May, 1889; acting
native commissioner, Makoni district,
15th June, 1900.

HULLEY, THOMAS BENJAMIN (L).—
Native commissioner, Mazoe, 1st April,
1895; native commissioner, Lo Mo-
gundi, May, 1895; clerk to chief
native commissioner, June, 1895;
native commissioner, Melsetter, September, 1895; O.C. Umtali burghers,
1896; native commissioner, Umtali
district, 19th June, 1896; assistant
magistrate, Umtali, and J.P. for
Southern Rhodesia, 22nd March, 1900.

HUNT, ALBERT CHARLES.—Postal
assistant, England, January, 1893;
entered Rhodesian service, 25th March,
1898.

HUNT, JOHN GOLDSWORTHY.—Telegraph department, England, October,
1892; entered Cape service as telegraphist, 21st September, 1895;
entered Rhodesian service as telegraphist, 2nd October, 1896; principal
clerk, telegraph audit, 9th October,
1900.

HUNT, PERCIVAL GEORGE.—Telegraph department, England, September, 1894; entered Westralian service
as telegraphist, 22nd August, 1896;
entered Rhodesian service as telegraphist, 6th May, 1897.

HUNTLY, GORDON MERRIMAN (L).
—Clerk to magistrate, Hanover, Cape
Colony, 10th April, 1878; transferred
to Queenstown, July, 1879; clerk to
civil commissioner, Kimberley, September, 1881; assistant examiner of
accounts, audit office, Capetown, April,
1882; chief accountant, British Bechuanaland, October, 1885; examiner of
Bechuanaland accounts in high commissioner's office, Capetown, January,
1887; resigned appointment, April,
1889; appointed to administrator's
office, British Bechuanaland, June,
1890; chief clerk to colonial secretary
and receiver-general, March, 1891, also
local representative of the B.S.A. Company; acted on various occasions as
colonial secretary and receiver-general
of British Bechuanaland, ; acted as secretary to H.H. the administrator of
British Bechuanaland from January,
1894 until annexation of territory to
Cape Colony in November, 1895; appointed to deeds registry office, Salisbury, Rhodesia, 20th February, 1898;
acting registrar of deeds and acting
sheriff of Rhodesia, April, 1898; acting
civil commissioner and magistrate, Victoria, November, 1898; appointed C.C.
and magistrate, Victoria, August,
1900.

HYLAND, PATRICK. — Entered
B.S.A.P., March, 1890; regt. sergt.-
major, M.F.F., 1896; garrison sergt.-
major, B.S.A.P., 1896; chief gaoler,
Salisbury, January 1st, 1897.

JACKSON, Hugh Marrison Gower. (L.).—Was eight and a half years in Natal civil service; appointed native commissioner, Matabeleland, 14th October, 1895; served as lieutenant, Gifford's horse, in Matabele rebellion, 1896 (medal); justice of the peace, 1897; special J.P., 29th June, 1900.

JACKSON, Staley Nettleship Gower (L.).—Was selected as one of escort to chief commissioner, Zululand, on the annexation of Amatongoland and Zambaan territories: appointed native commissioner, Matabeleland, 1st November, 1895; justice of the peace, 1897; served in Matabele rebellion, 1896 (medal).

JAMES, George Herbert.—Twelve years in the English civil service (secretary's office, general post office); clerk, mines department, 19th June, 1899.

JEAREY, John George.—Served in Langeberg campaign, 1897; appointed to chief secretary's office, Salisbury, on 29th November, 1897.

JENNINGS, William.—Telegraphist, England, 1890; telegraphist, Rhodesia, 5th April, 1896; postmaster, Palapye, 7th April, 1897; postmaster, Palapye station, 1st February, 1900; telegraphist, Bulawayo, 1st September, 1901.

JONES, Alfred Francis.—Late trooper, M.R.F.; joined transport department as conductor, 22nd July, 1897; issuer, 1st September, 1897; clerk, 1st April, 1899.

JONES, Llewellyn Powys (L.)—Registrar to Mr. Justice Dwyer, 1st December, 1879; clerk, Paarl, 8th March, 1881; magistrate's office, Capetown, 1stMarch, 1885, and Queenstown, 16th October, 1885; second class clerk, Barkly West, June, 1886; assistant resident magistrate, Barkly, July, 1886; acting civil commissioner and resident magistrate, 28th May, 1888, and acting resident magistrate, Beaconsfield, 1890; Kimberley, October, 1890; transferred to Oudtshoorn as assistant magistrate,

August, 1891; assistant magistrate Capetown, and assistant lay superintendent, Robben Island, November, 1892; acting magistrate, Molteno, December, 1895; assistant magistrate, Albany, 7th March, 1896; transferred Rhodesia civil service as magistrate, Bulawayo, on 28th February, 1897.

JUDSON, Daniel.—Junior assistant Capetown, 1882; broke service for five months while serving with the Warren expedition in Bechuanaland; rejoined Cape service, October, 1885; Transvaal postal service, 1887; assistant, Kimberley, November, 1889; entered Rhodesian service as inspector of telegraphs, October, 1893; surveyor and district engineer, Bulawayo, 1st November, 1897.

KENNEDY, James Hutchinson.—Service of 12 years under the Griqualand West and Cape colonial government; chief accountant in Mashonaland, 1st September, 1891; master and registrar, high court of Southern Rhodesia, 1st November, 1894; acted as judge of the high court, August, 1895; served as chief commissariat officer during Matabele war, 1893, and as B.S.A. Company's agent and transport officer at Mafeking, Bechuanaland, during the native rebellion, 1896 (war medal and clasp); chairman, tender board, March, 1900; high sheriff, August, 1900; appointed a member of legislative council, June, 1901.

KENNY, Edward Thomas.—Joined M.M.P., April, 1892; interpreter to magistrate and high court, Salisbury, March, 1895; registrar of natives, Salisbury, March, 1897; acting native commissioner, South Mazoe, 7th October, 1896; inspector of natives, Northern Mazoe, July, 1898.

KING, Godfrey James.—Clerk in administrator's office, February, 1895; transferred as clerk in deeds office, August, 1895; acting registrar of deeds and companies, October, 1895; registrar of deeds and companies, 1st April, 1897; registrar of patents, 6th

July, 1897; acting high sheriff, August, 1897, November, 1898, March, 1899, May, 1900; acting under secretary, 25th April to 4th July, 1899.

KOTZE, JOHN GILBERT. – Born at Capetown, November 5th, 1849; educated at the South African College; graduated in law at the university of London, January, 1873; obtained senior exhibition in common law at the inns of court, June, 1872, and called to the bar by the honourable society of the Inner Temple, April, 1874; practised at the bar of the supreme and eastern districts courts, Cape Colony; appointed judge of the high court of the Transvaal Province during the period of British annexation, May, 1877; appointed member of commission for investigation of claims for compensation during the war, 1880-81, under Pretoria convention; appointed chief justice of the high court of the Transvaal (South African Republic) on the retrocession of the country, August, 1881, which appointment held until February, 1898; was chairman of the board of public examiners in literature and science, 1890-98; edited the statute law of the Transvaal (1849-87) and three volumes of reports of cases decided in the high court of that state; has also translated *Van Leuwen's Commentaries on Roman-Dutch Law* in two volumes; is a knight grand cross of the Portuguese order of the Conception; appointed attorney general of Southern Rhodesia, and member of the executive and legislative councils of the province, August, 1900.

KRIGE, WILLEM ADOLPH. – Clerk Capetown office, November, 1895; clerk to chief accountant, Salisbury, December, 1896; acting superintendent, stationery department, June, 1899; chief accountant's office, April, 1900.

LAESSOE, HEROLD HENRY ABRAHAMSON (L). – Appointed clerk, native department, Matabeleland, 19th February, 1900; was formerly in the B.S.A.

police from the 5th November, 1896, to 5th November, 1897.

LAING, WILLIAM THOMSON (L). – Clerk, high sheriff's office, Capetown, 18th February, 1895; clerk to registrar of the Eastern Districts court, Grahamstown, 21st August, 1896; relieving clerk, civil commissioner's office, Grahamstown, 3rd January, 1898, to 27th April, 1898; relieving clerk, resident magistrate's office, Queenstown, 27th July, 1898, to 1st October, 1898; relieving clerk, resident magistrate's office, Richmond, 1st to 31st January, 1899; transferred to Rhodesia as examiner of accounts, 1st May, 1899; acting secretary to the tender board, Salisbury, 19th February, 1900, to 4th March, 1900.

LAMBERT, ALEXANDER JAMES. – Telegraph line, Cape Colony, 1st February, 1889; lineman, Rhodesia, 1st August, 1895.

LANNING, ROBERT. – Civil service, Basutoland, 1894; assistant native commissioner, Matabeleland, 1st September, 1895; native commissioner, 4th November, 1896; served in Matabeleland rebellion, 1896 (medal); J.P., Bulawayo.

LAPHAM, THOMAS URIAH. – Telegraphist, England, 7th August, 1887; entered Cape service as telegraphist, 1st December, 1893; entered Rhodesian service as telegraphist, 8th December, 1894; postmaster, 24th April, 1897.

LAURIE, CHARLES GEORGE. – Claim inspector, mines department, 1st June, 1895; clerk, public works department, 1st December, 1898; chief clerk, 5th June, 1900.

LAWLEY, HIS EXCELLENCY CAPTAIN THE HON. SIR ARTHUR, K.C.M.G. – Lieutenant, 10th Royal Hussars, 1882; retired with rank of captain, 1892; appointed secretary to administrator (Earl Grey) in May, 1896; deputy administrator of Matabeleland, Nov., 1896; administrator of Matabeleland, Dec., 1898; acted as administrator of Mashonaland from July, 1899; is a justice of the peace for Southern Rhodesia ; appointed governor West Australia, January, 1901.

LAWLOR, EDWARD JAMES (L).— Joined the M.M. police, 1st April, 1895, to 31st March, 1896 : appointed assistant clerk to the magistrate, Salisbury, 11th April, 1898 ; clerk in law department, 1st August, 1898 : acting assistant magistrate, Gwelo, 1st March, 1900 ; assistant magistrate, Bulawayo, 1st November, 1900: acting magistrate and civil commissioner, Tuli, 13th December, 1900, to 23rd January, 1901.

LAWSON, WILLIAM.— Clerk in commissariat store, 1st October, 1896 ; commissariat storekeeper, 1st January, 1897.

LE SUEUR, GORDON WILLIAM (L). —Clerk in office of engineer-in-chief, Cape government railways, 29th December, 1892 ; transferred to office of general manager of railways, 1st February, 1893 : transferred to colonial secretary's office, 21st February, 1893 ; second-class clerk, 1st January, 1897 ; transferred to civil service of Rhodesia, 9th June, 1897 ; detailed for special service until August, 1898 ; magistrate's office, Bulawayo, 29th August, 1898 ; acting assistant magistrate, Bulawayo, 1st April, 1899 ; assistant magistrate, 5th October, 1899 ; justice of the peace for Southern Rhodesia ; acting senior clerk, chief secretary's office, 1st October, 1901.

LEWIS, DAVID MORRALL. — 2nd lieutenant, 4th batt. Royal Welsh Fusiliers from 1888 to 1889 ; B.S.A. Co.'s Police, March to November, 1891 ; joined B.S.A. Co. volunteer force raised in Natal, April 27th, 1896 : served throughout the Mashonaland rebellion, 1896 and 1897 (entitled to medal) : joined the Mashonaland constabulary (Mashonaland municipal police) on April 22nd, 1897 : sub-inspector, 1900.

LINGARD, MARK ALEXANDER.— Joined B.S.A. police, 1890 ; appointed

assistant commissary officer at Hartley, September, 1891 ; secretary to P.M.G., May, 1892 ; postmaster, Victoria, May, 1893 ; served with Victoria column through Matabele war, 1893 ; clerk of the court and registrar of natives, May, 1894: clerk, native department, June, 1895 : appointed clerk agricultural department and registrar of brands, April, 1897.

LISTER, HENRY CORYTON.—Clerk in D.A.A.G.'s office, Bulawayo, 20th June, 1896 ; transferred to controller's office, 7th October, 1896 ; appointed O.C. transport, 1st February, 1897.

LONGDEN, WILLIAM MATTHIAS.— Civil commissioner and magistrate : joined company's service, June, 1891 : obtained land concession for B.S.A. company from Gungunyama, king of Gazaland, September, 1891 ; employed on special service in Gazaland, 1892 and 1893 ; appointed controller of stores, Tuli, 1893 : served in Matabele war, 1893 (special service medal) ; had charge of special mission to Gaza king, 1894 ; appointed company's representative, Tuli, 1894, and civil commissioner and magistrate, Tuli, 1895 ; acting magistrate, Victoria, August, 1895 ; civil commissioner and magistrate, Melsetter, October, 1895, and commanded Melsetter burghers native rebellion, 1896 : J.P. for Rhodesia, January, 1897.

LOW, WILLIAM.—Waterlow & Sons, ltd., shipping department, London, January 7th, 1895 : joined as clerk B.S.A. Co., stationery department, August 4th, 1900.

MACEY, WILLIAM HENRY.—Telegraphist, Rhodesia, 16th October, 1896 ; postmaster, Victoria, 22nd December, 1899 ; acting postmaster, Kopje, 27th July, 1900 : postmaster, Enkeldoorn, 15th March, 1901.

MACDOUGALL, JAMES WILLIAM.— Madras police, Nov., 1885 ; joined Matabeleland mounted police, 1st Dec., 1894 ; transferred to municipal police,

18th Jan., 1895; appointed sub-inspector, 6th Oct., 1898; served through 1896 rebellion (medal).

MACGLASHAN, Neil. — Mining commissioner, Manica, 1890; registrar of claims, 1895; mining commissioner, Bulawayo, 5th October, 1897.

MATHEWS, Charles Joseph. — Assistant on survey of the township of Salisbury, Jan., 1892; entered the B.S.A. co.'s drawing office, July, 1892; appointed chief draughtsman, March, 1895.

MATTHEWS, Arthur Holland. — Passed theoretical survey examination, June, 1899; clerk and assistant to examiner of diagrams, surveyor general's office, 18th September, 1899.

McCULLOCH, Godfrey Henry (L). —Clerk to civil commissioner and magistrate, Victoria, 30th January, 1895; government representative, Enkeldoorn, 10th Dec., 1897; special J.P., Enkeldoorn, 1st July, 1898; assistant magistrate, Enkeldoorn, 1st Nov., 1898; assistant magistrate, Salisbury, 1st May, 1901.

McGIBBONY, John. — Victorian postal service, September, 1889; West Australia, August, 1896; Rhodesia, postal assistant, 22nd May, 1900.

McILWAINE, H.—Clerk to magistrate, Salisbury, December, 1898; clerk of the court, Salisbury, February, 1900; transferred to master's office, high court, July, 1901; has also acted as clerk to the legal adviser.

McILWAINE, Robert.—M.A. and LL.B., Ireland; appointed clerk to magistrate, Knysna, 7th December, 1895; clerk magistrate's office, Capetown, 7th July, 1897; clerk attorney-general's office, and assistant secretary, civil service commission, 3rd December, 1897; secretary, civil service commission, 14th January, 1898; passed special examination in Dutch language; sometime examiner for Cape civil service commission; transferred to the British South Africa company's service, 1st October, 1898,

and appointed assistant magistrate, Salisbury, from that date; appointed chief clerk, judicial branch, chief secretary's office, 1st July, 1899; has acted as magistrate, Victoria, Umtali, Enkeldoorn and Salisbury, as secretary to the law department, and as inspector of schools for Southern Rhodesia, and statist; is author of " Instructions for Special Justices of the Peace in Southern Rhodesia."

MEDCALF, Frederick George.— Junior clerk, Cape government railways, May, 1892; trooper, Matabeleland mounted police, January, 1895; assistant, telegraph message branch, Capetown, February, 1896; to Rhodesian service, as postmaster, Mochudi, 1st May, 1896; postal assistant, from 1st August, 1896; audit clerk, telegraph message branch, Salisbury, 27th May, 1900; postmaster at Enkeldoorn, 1st July, 1900; postmaster at Gwelo, 17th July, 1900.

MEE, Edwin Bakewell Osborne.— Postal and telegraph department, Orange Free State, 1st June, 1890; postal assistant, Rhodesia, 1st October, 1899.

MEREDITH, Llewellyn Cambria. —F.C., Mangwendi district, April, 1893; N.C., Makoni district, November, 1894; N.C., Charter district, May, 1895; N.C., Melsetter, 1st November, 1895.

MILES, Herbert Picton.—Clerk to civil commissioner and magistrate, Umtali, 2nd May, 1896; clerk of court, 1st October, 1901.

MILTON, His Honour William Henry, C.M.G.—Cape civil service, 1878 to 1896; officiating clerk to the executive council, Cape Colony, 1885; acting secretary, prime minister's department, 1890; private secretary to the Right Hon. C. J. Rhodes, prime minister, from 1st July, 1891; chief clerk and chief accountant, colonial secretary's office, 1st December, 1891; secretary to the prime minister, 8th March, 1894; detached from Cape civil service for service in Rhodesia, August, 1896 ; appointed chief secretary, and secretary native affairs, September, 1896 ; acting administrator of Southern Rhodesia, July, 1897 ; administrator of Mashonaland and senior administrator of Southern Rhodesia, 3rd December, 1898. Is also president of the executive and legislative councils.

MONRO, CLAUDE FREDERICK HUGH.— Private secretary in house of commons to contractor for parliamentary debates ; clerk, mines department, 29th August, 1900.

MONTAGU, ERNEST WILLIAM SAUNDERS. - Eight years in Cape civil service ; clerk, mines department, 16th July, 1898 ; registrar of claims, 2nd April, 1899.

MOODIE, DONALD HARRY.—Cape civil service, Feb., 1888 ; clerk, chief magistrate's office, Kokstad, 1887 ; R.M. clerk. Mt. Fletcher, 1892 ; clerk to R.M., Matatiele, 1893 ; clerk to R.M., Umzimkulu, 1895 ; justice of the peace for East Griqualand, and has frequently acted as magistrate ; appointed native commissioner, Matabeleland, November, 1896 ; special J.P., 3rd February, 1899 ; native commissioner, N'danga, 15th November, 1900.

MORRIS, ERNEST WALTER.—Cattle inspector, Bulawayo, March, 1896 ; native commissioner, Marandella, 1st October, 1896 ; acting as native commissioner, M'rewa's, 3rd April, 1901.

MORRIS, STANLEY FREDERIC.—Appointed clerk, Mafeking, August, 1896 ; company's agent at Mochudi, Palapye, Francistown, during 1897 ; assistant, controller's office, November, 1897 ; transferred to chief accountant's office, March, 1898.

MOSS, GEORGE ERNEST. — 2nd officer of customs, St. Helena, 1st September, 1896 ; acting supervisor of customs, 1st December, 1897, to 1st February, 1898 ; clerk in colonial secretary's office, Capetown, 23rd April,

1900 ; statistical clerk, customs department, 6th September, 1900 ; officer in charge customs, Plumtree, 16th April, 1901 ; 2nd examining officer, Bulawayo, 1st October, 1901.

MYBURGH, PETER DENYSSEN.— Clerk, chief accountant's department, 1st February, 1897 ; appointed clerk, civil commissioner, Salisbury, 1st November, 1898.

MYBURGH, RYK H. (L).—Temporary clerk, commissioner of crown lands and public works office, March, 1882 ; resigned, September, 1883 ; clerk, colonial secretary's office, January, 1885 ; clerk to civil commissioner and resident magistrate, Riversdale, October, 1885; Stellenbosch, April, 1887 ; Paarl (acting), March, 1889 ; magistrate's office, Capetown, May, 1890 ; Wynberg, July, 1890 ; acting magistrate, Wynberg and acting visiting magistrate, Tokai and Constantia convict stations and Porter reformatory, occasionally, 1892-96 ; transferred Rhodesia civil service, 1st October, 1898 ; assistant magistrate, Umtali, October, 1898 ; civil commissioner and magistrate, Umtali, January, 1899.

NELL, ARTHUR.—Clerk, civil commissioner's office, Bulawayo, 8th March, 1896 ; accountant to civil commissioner, 1st August, 1897.

NEVETT, JOHN HENRY.—Postal department, England, July, 1890 ; entered Cape service as telelegraphist, 16th November, 1895 ; entered Rhodesian service as telegraphist, 1st October, 1898.

NEWNHAM, ARTHUR HENRY.—Appointed native commissioner, Melsetter, 26th April, 1895 ; resigned service, 1st October, 1895 ; rejoined and appointed district medical officer, Hartley, 17th November, 1895 ; clerk, public works department, 6th January, 1898 ; transferred as clerk in stationery department, 1st April, 1899 ; audit office, 1st April, 1901.

NORRIS, SISSON BROOKE.—Clerk, surveyor general's office, 1st June,

1894 ; clerk in the administrator's and public prosecutor's offices ; clerk, mines department, 1st April, 1895.

OGILVIE, OGILVIE HOLLINGS.— Claim inspector, 1st June, 1895 ; acting mining commissioner, 28th February, 1897 ; mining commissioner, 1st April, 1898.

O'LEARY, DANIEL MARTIN.—Telegraph department, West Australia, December, 1896 ; post assistant, Rhodesia, 22nd May, 1900.

OLIPHANT, STEWART JAMES.— Joined Cape public works department as draughtsman, 11th September, 1889 : was clerk of works at several stations : assistant clerk of works, new post office, Capetown ; transferred to B.S.A. Company's civil service, 9th May, 1899 ; inspector of public works, 1st August, 1899.

OLIVE, WILLIAM. — Clerk in accounting department, Cape government railways, August, 1889 ; principal clerk, statistical branch, 1891 ; transferred to Pretoria in charge clearing office, October, 1893 ; transferred to Orange Free State railway service as clearing officer, Pretoria, January, 1897 : appointed accountant, B.S.A. Company, Capetown, June, 1898 ; acting representative of company at Capetown, June, 1899 ; is also accountant to Bechuanaland railway company.

ORPEN, JOSEPH MILLERD.—Appointed J.P. and government land surveyor, 1851, and served as lieutenant of volunteers in the kafir war of that year : elected member of the assembly of delegates, Orange River sovereignty, 1853 ; member of the 1st elected Orange Free State Volksraad, 1854 ; appointed landdrost of Winburg and Harrismith the same year ; commanded the Free State forces in expedition against "Witsi," 1856 ; elected member for Queenstown, 1871 ; after the dissolution in 1873 was appointed first chief magistrate and British resident in the territories now called Griqualand

East and Pondoland ; on the Langalibalele outbreak in Natal raised and led a force into and through Basutoland in the operations which led to the surrender of that chief ; resigned in 1875 : engaged on survey of Griqualand West when rebellion broke out, raised and was appointed captain of corps of guides and placed on staff as chief of intelligence department : appointed major and acting civil commissioner of district of Hay, the seat of rebellion ; re-elected as member of Aliwal North, 1878, until at close of Basuto rebellion appointed acting governor's agent, retired 1883 ; twice re-elected member for Wodehouse (C.C.) ; appointed 5th January, 1897, to the charge of the department of lands and agriculture, Rhodesia, with seat on executive council with title of surveyor general ; now holds official seat as member of legislative council.

OSBORNE, HENRY JAMES.—Inspector of telegraphs, Pretoria, 22nd November, 1881 ; entered Cape service as lineman at Vryburg, 1st February, 1887 : to Mafeking in charge of base depot, 15th April, 1890 ; entered Rhodesian service as maintenance officer at Mochudi, 1st March, 1891 : sub-inspector at Mochudi, 6th December, 1896 : maintenance officer at Macloutsie, 27th June, 1898.

PEEL, ALFRED MICHAEL JOHN RUSSEL.—Joined the British South Africa police in December, 1896 : served during the Mashona rebellion, 1897 (medal) : transport department, January, 1898 ; clerk to magistrate, Salisbury, 1st April, 1899 ; served in Transvaal war with Rhodesia Regiment, 1900.

PETT, ALFRED GEORGE. Clerk, C.C. office, Cradock, 13th February, 1891 ; census office, 28th June, 1891 ; C.C. office, Capetown, December, 1891 ; C.C. and R.M. office, Sutherland, May, 1892 ; C.C. office, Clanwilliam, December, 1892 ; C.C. office, Paarl, June, 1895 ; C.C. office, Aliwal North, August

1895 ; colonial secretary's office (convict branch), September, 1895 ; accounting branch, April, 1896 ; transferred to Rhodesia as examiner of accounts, in charge of pension and guarantee funds, March, 1898 ; chief examiner of accounts, April, 1899 ; acting civil commissioner, Salisbury, 15th February to 19th September, 1901.

PIDCOCK, CHARLES ALEXANDER.—Barrister-at-law ; assistant magistrate, Bulawayo, 27th October, 1897 ; acting magistrate, Tuli, 5th July, 1900.

POSSELT, JOHN WILLIAM. — Formerly in Natal civil service; appointed assistant native commissioner, Matabeleland, 15th April, 1897 ; justice of the peace.

POWELL, JOHN PETER ARTON.—Entered Cape railway department, 16th July, 1876 ; postmaster, 1883 ; special justice of the peace and issuer process, De Aar, 1893; entered Rhodesian service, 6th March, 1896, as postal assistant ; postmaster, Bulawayo, 1st August, 1897.

POWER, JAMES ROBERT. — Postal department, United Kingdom, June, 1896 ; post assistant, Rhodesia, 4th May, 1899 ; postmaster, Palapye, June, 1901.

PREW, ARTHUR WILLIAM BROWNE.—Telegraph department, England, 16th September, 1894 ; entered West Australian service, 22nd August, 1896 ; entered Rhodesian postal service, 14th November, 1898 ; T.M.B., 1st February, 1899

QUIN, HENRY CHARLES.—Clerk to C.C. and M., Gwelo, 1st September, 1895 ; acting C.C. and M., Gwelo, during March, 1897, and at Tuli from May to July, 1898.

RANGELEY, HENRY (L).—Joined Matabeleland constabulary, May 11th, 1897, and acted as police prosecutor, magistrate's court, from January, 1899 ; appointed magistrate's office, Bulawayo, as clerk and to assist in prosecuting in the court, September 1st, 1900.

RANKINE, ANDREW BOGIE.—Post office, January, 1894 ; master's office May, 1894 ; assistant registrar, 1896 ; chief clerk (general branch), chief secretary's office, July, 1899 ; served in Matabele war, 1893 (medal) ; Mashonaland, 1896 (clasp) ; has twice acted as master of the high court, from September, 1895, to December, 1896, and December, 1897, to November, 1898.

REDFERN, ARTHUR WILLIAM. — Served with the Matabeleland relief force, 1896 (medal and clasp) ; clerk, stationery department, April, 1898 ; transferred to chief accountant's office, November, 1898, and to master's office, July, 1899.

REDMOND, VIVIAN.—Cape railway department, November, 1896 ; postal assistant, Rhodesia, 8th January, 1900.

RICE, FRANK. — Joined Bulawayo municipal police force, 23rd January, 1895 ; transferred Mashonaland division Umtali municipal police, 15th January, 1896 ; appointed sub-inspector, Bulawayo municipal police, 25th April, 1898 ; served in Umtali burgher force during 1896 rebellion (medal) ; inspector, Southern Rhodesia constabulary, 1st January, 1901.

RIVERS, CHARLES HARDCASTLE.—B.A. Cambridge ; government surveyor ; surveyor to mines department, 19th July, 1900.

ROBERTS, GEORGE.—Entered Rhodesian service as telegraphist, 21st February, 1896 ; chief telegraphist, Bulawayo, 1st January, 1897 ; chief telegraphist, Salisbury, 15th September, 1898 ; seconded for service with African transcontinental telegraph company as superintendent of telegraphs, 1st February, 1899 ; superintendent of Bulawayo telegraph office, 1st November, 1899.

ROBERTS, LEONARD FAREWELL HOLSTOK.—Appointed temporarily as clerk to C.C. and M., Victoria, in June,

1898 ; appointed as clerk to C.C. and M., Melsetter, 1st January, 1899.

ROBERTSON, JAMES. ---Administrator's office, Salisbury, December, 1895 ; acted as secretary to the administrator from April, 1896, to September, 1897 ; Mashona rebellion, 1896-7 (medal) ; acting under secretary from 26th April, 1898, to June, 1898, and from 31st January to 1st May, 1899 ; acting government representative, Enkeldoorn, June, 1898 ; clerk to the legislative and executive councils, 1st May, 1899.

ROBINSON, LEO GEORGE.---Clerk in chief native commissioner's office, Bulawayo, 1st February, 1897 : assistant native commissioner, 1st July, 1897 : justice of the peace.

ROSS, ARCHAR RUSSELL.—Appointed native commissioner, Makoni district, 20th April, 1895 ; on special service purchasing cattle in Australia, 1900.

SAWERTHAL, HENRY GEORGE EMANUEL JULIUS EDWARD.—Draughtsman, public works, Queenstown, Cape Colony, May, 1882 ; assistant surveyor on Tembuland commission, August, 1882 ; computer, royal observatory, Cape of Good Hope, July, 1885 , assistant surveyor, Bechuanaland railway extension, August, 1890 ; assistant to surveyor general, Mashonaland, September, 1891 ; B.S.A. co.'s representative, Umtali, June to August, 1896 ; acting assistant surveyor general, January, 1897 : has twice acted as surveyor general ; acting examiner of diagrams, 28th February, 1901.

SCANLEN, THE HONOURABLE SIR THOMAS CHARLES, K.C.M.G.— Member for the Cradock district in the Cape house of assembly from 1870 to 1896 ; J.P. for the districts of Cape and Cradock ; prime minister and attorney general of Cape Colony, 1881 ; prime minister and colonial secretary, 1882 ; member of divisional council of Cradock, also chairman of the municipality ; appointed legal adviser to B.S.A. co.,

October, 1894 ; member of executive council, January, 1896 ; acting public prosecutor, April, 1896 ; president of compensation board, September, 1896 ; senior member of executive council, 20th December, 1896 ; acting administrator, December, 1898 ; member of legislative council, May, 1899 ; has on several occasions acted as company's representative.

SCOTT, WILLIAM EDWARD EDWARDS.—Appointed assistant native commissioner, Umtali, May, 1896 ; native commissioner, Hartley district, 1st April, 1897.

SHAND, WILLIAM ROBERTSON (L).---Clerk, Knysna, 17th April, 1888 ; Swellendam, September, 1888 ; assistant magistrate, Willowmore, 1st August, 1890 ; Glen Grey, 2nd April, 1893 ; transferred to Rhodesian service as assistant magistrate, Gwelo, 1st October, 1898 ; has acted as civil commissioner and resident magistrate in the Cape Colony at various times ; has acted as assistant magistrate at Enkeldoorn and Bulawayo, and as magistrate at Gwelo.

SHARP, ERNEST CHAPPEL.—Clerk in the surveyor general's office, 1st April, 1894 ; appointed acting assistant registrar, high court, 18th February, 1896 ; served in Matabeleland and Mashonaland rebellions until 1st September, 1896 ; secretary to assessment of compensation board, September, 7th, 1896 ; acting high sheriff and chief clerk to public prosecutor on September 7th, 1896 ; justice of the peace for Southern Rhodesia ; assistant statist, March, 1897 ; clerk to civil commissioner, Salisbury, April 4th, 1900.

SHORT, GEORGE. — O.R., sergt., Mount Darwin patrol, 1897 ; temporary clerk, chief accountant's department, 7th March, 1898 ; assistant bookkeeper, 1st April, 1899.

SINCLAIR, ALEXANDER.---Victorian postal department, November, 1891 ; telegraphist, Rhodesia, 11th April, 1900.

SMITH, EDWARD DUFFUS. Clerk in pay office, Bulawayo, 1st June, 1896 ; transferred to controller's office, Salisbury, 1st May, 1897 ; promoted to accountant for the controller's department, Mashonaland, 1st April, 1898 ; clerk in charge, stores department, Salisbury, 1st July, 1901.

SMITH, FERGUS JARDINE MENZIES. —Clerk, administrator's office, Bulawayo, January 9th, 1899 ; civil commissioner's office, Bulawayo, July 1st, 1901.

SMITH, FREDERICK WILLIAM. — Joined Cape government service, 10th June, 1881 ; Cape mounted police, 16th January, 1883 ; winner of the 1st prize essay on colonial police administration, 27th June, 1885 ; appointed chief constable, Kingwilliamstown 19th November, 1885 ; appointed superintendent of the Kingwilliamstown borough police force, 8th March, 1888 ; justice of the peace, 20th December, 1889 ; selected by the Cape government to reorganise the Port Elizabeth police department, 1st January, 1895 ; returned afterwards to Kingwilliamstown ; seconded for service in Matabeleland to reorganise municipal police, 1st July, 1898 ; justice of the peace for Rhodesia, 27th July, 1898 ; transferred as inspector commanding municipal police and head of detective department, Matabeleland, 24th November, 1898.

SMITH, PERCY GEORGE (L).—Clerk, chief accountant, Cape railways, January, 1889 ; clerk to engineer in chief, Cape railways, 1889 ; magistrate's clerk, Kimberley, 1892 ; assistant magistrate, Douglass, 1893 ; additional magistrate, Bulawayo, July, 1894 ; magistrate, Bulawayo, July, 1896 ; C.C. and M., Gwelo, July, 1897.

SMITH WRIGHT, EDWARD HENRY. —Appointed clerk, general stores, in July, 1895 ; clerk, statist's department September, 1895 ; clerk, magistrate's court, January, 1896 ; clerk, accountant's department, October, 1896 ; examiner of accounts, audit department, October, 1897 ; secretary tender board, Salisbury, November, 1898 ; acting chief examiner of accounts, 15th February, 1901.

SPEIGHT, ARTHUR EDWIN (L).— Clerk, Bechuanaland customs, Mafeking, 10th October, 1895 ; transferred to customs, East London, June, 1898 ; transferred to Southern Rhodesia customs, Umtali, 9th July, 1899 ; acting sub-collector, Umtali, 12th February, 1900 ; clerk, customs administrative branch, December, 1900 ; chief examining officer, Bulawayo, 16th April, 1901.

SPRECKLEY, HARRY UNWIN.— Clerk to C.C. and M.C., Mazoe, August, 1895 ; clerk to C.C., Salisbury, October, 1896 ; clerk, mines department, October, 1897.

SPRIGG, WILLIAM PORTER.—Clerk, Castle mail packet company, 1891 ; private secretary to Sir Gordon Sprigg, 1897 ; forwarding clerk, Capetown office, January, 1898,

STEVENS, JOHN ALFRED.—Sent on special mission to Gazaland, 1890 ; joined Capetown office of B.S.A. Company, March, 1891, as head of correspondence department ; acted as secretary from October, 1894, to April, 1895 ; appointed acting secretary, Capetown, January, 1896 ; is also secretary to Bechuanaland railway company.

STEWART, DUDLEY WARREN.— Joined the north-west mounted police, Canada, 1st July, 1890 ; Cape mounted rifles, 10th May, 1894 ; joined Mashonaland mounted police, 28th November, 1895 ; transferred into Mashonaland municipal police, 18th November, 1896 ; appointed sub-inspector, 21st August, 1898, and transferred into Matabeleland division ; served through 1896 rebellion (medal).

STEWART, WILLIAM DYKES. — Clerk to legal adviser, 15th September, 1898 ; public prosecutor's office,

1st May, 1900; attorney general's office, 1st August, 1900.

STIDOLPH, ALAN. — Assistant draughtsman, public works department, Capetown, 1897-98 ; appointed assistant draughtsman in surveyor general's office, 16th January, 1899.

STUART, CHARLES TRAVERS.— Clerk and public prosecutor in magistrate's court, Nqutu, Zululand ; sworn interpreter in the Zulu language ; appointed native commissioner, Matabeleland, 1st November, 1896 ; served on commission to draft code for native law for Matabeleland, 1898 ; special justice of the peace, 3rd February, 1899.

STUART, PHILIP ARNOLD (L.).— Formerly in Natal civil service ; appointed acting assistant native commissioner, Matabeleland, 7th September, 1897 ; assistant native commissioner, 25th September, 1898 ; justice of the peace.

SYMONS, SAMUEL MARSHALL.—Post office (Taunton, England), 1893 ; transferred to Cape service (Capetown) 21st September, 1895 ; entered Rhodesian service, post office, Bulawayo, 20th September, 1896 : post office, Salisbury, 20th May, 1897 ; surveyor general's office, 1st January, 1898 ; clerk, customs department, Salisbury, 1st August, 1899.

TABERER, HENRY MELVILLE, B.A., Oxon.—Clerk to secretary for Zululand, September, 1893 ; secretary for Zululand (acting), January, 1894 : secretary for Zululand, June, 1894 ; acting magistrate, Echowe, Zululand, March, 18'5 ; assistant chief native commissioner, Mashonaland, June, 1895 ; chief native commissioner, Mashonaland, November, 1895 : controller of cattle, Rhodesia, April, 1896 ; O.C. "C" troop, Umtali volunteers, June-December, 1896 ; O.C. transport and supplies August-December, 1896 ; acting magistrate and civil commissioner, Umtali, November, 1896.

TABERER, WALTER STRINGFELLOW (L).—Clerk to special magistrate, Kingwilliamstown, July, 1891 ; clerk to civil commissioner and resident magistrate, Kingwilliamstown, 16th January, 1895 ; clerk to civil commissioner and resident magistrate, Barkly West, 4th January, 1896 ; joined native department, Mashonaland, 1st January, 1897 ; assistant chief native commissioner, Mashonaland, 5th July, 1898.

TAYLOR, HERBERT JOHN. — Appointed native commissioner for Matabeleland, 1st October, 1894 ; chief native commissioner and justice of the peace, 1st May, 1895 ; captain of "M" troop, B.F.F. corps, April, 1896 ; served in Matabele rebellion (medal), mentioned in despatches ; captain, Southern Rhodesia volunteers, 18th August, 1899.

THERON, HARRY FRANCIS.—Cape telegraph department, June, 1890 ; entered Rhodesian service as telegraphist, December, 1895 ; postmaster, Selukwe, January, 1896 ; postmaster, Gwelo, June, 1896 ; resigned, June, 1897 ; rejoined Rhodesian service as telegraphist at Victoria, June, 1898 ; postmaster, Selukwe, September, 1898 ; assistant, Salisbury, September, 1900.

THOMAS, MORGAN THOMAS (L).— Appointed assistant native commissioner, Matabeleland, 1st March, 1897 ; justice of the peace.

THOMAS, WILLIAM ELLIOTT (L).— Appointed native commissioner, Matabeleland, 1st March, 1895 ; served in Matabele rebellion, 1896 (medal) ; special justice of the peace, 3rd February, 1899 ; has on three occasions acted as chief native commissioner, Matabeleland.

TILNEY, WILLIAM ANDERSON.— Assistant native commissioner, Matabeleland, 4th June, 1897 ; acting N.C. 12th October, 1897 ; acting registrar of natives, Bulawayo, 17th January, 1898 ; justice of the peace, 1898.

TOBILCOCK, Thomas Henry Miners.—Telegraphist, Rhodesia, 28th April, 1900 ; transferred to G.P.O., Salisbury, as clerk, 1st December, 1900.

TONGE, Arthur Reginald.—Appointed clerk, deeds office, Bulawayo, 1st September, 1896 ;- registrar of deeds and companies for Matabeleland, 16th May, 1900 ; appointed J.P. for Southern Rhodesia, 1st November, 1900.

TOWNSEND, Edward Ross.—Chief clerk to postmaster general and superintendent of telegraphs, British Bechuanaland, May, 1889 ; clerk to registrar of deeds, British Bechuanaland, April, 1891 ; registrar of brands and clerk to registrar of deeds, British Bechuanaland, January, 1893 ; acting registrar of deeds, October, 1893, to March, 1894 ; assistant resident magistrate and clerk to civil commissioner, Mafeking ; justice of the peace for British Bechuanaland (acted as civil commissioner and resident magistrate 20th June to 31st July, 1894) May, 1894 ; registrar of deeds for Matabeleland, 3rd June, 1895 ; registrar of companies, Matabeleland, justice of the peace for Bulawayo, October, 1895 ; acting civil commissioner for Bulawayo and registrar of deeds, November, 1895 ; civil commissioner for Bulawayo, June, 1896 ; re-appointed registrar of deeds and companies, in addition to civil commissioner, April, 1897 ; acted as representative in Matabeleland of B.S.A. Company ; resigned appointment registrar of deeds and companies, Matabeleland, 21st July, 1899 ; secretary lands and agriculture, 1st April, 1901.

TREDGOLD, Clarkson Henry.—Barrister at law ; appointed representative of the public prosecutor at Bulawayo from 1st July, 1898 ; solicitor general, Southern Rhodesia, 1st September, 1900 ; acted as legal adviser from 20th May to 31st July, 1900 ; acted as attorney general from 1st December, 1900 ; appointed member of legislative council.

TUCKER, Walter Watson.—Appointed clerk to the postmaster general, Salisbury, August, 1896 ; transferred as clerk to the the registrar of deeds and companies, 1st July, 1897 ; acting registrar, 8th June, 1899.

TYLER, Alfred Edward. — Telegraphist, C.T.O., London, July, 1894 ; entered Cape service as postal assistant, 16th December, 1896 ; entered Rhodesian service as postal assistant, 5th August, 1898.

VINTCENT, Joseph.—B.A., LL.B. ; crown prosecutor for Bechuanaland, March, 1886 ; judge of the high court of Matabeleland, 10th September, 1894 ; president of the land commission established under the Matabeleland order in council, 1894 ; was a member of the council under such order ; acted as administrator for Southern Rhodesia from November, 1895, to November, 1896 ; is senior judge of the high court of Southern Rhodesia.

WADESON, Thomas James. — Inspector of explosives, weights and measures, board of trade, England, November, 1891, to March, 1897 ; served with S.R.V. under Col. Plumer, October, 1899, to July, 1900 ; clerk, customs department, Bulawayo, 1st September, 1900 ; examining officer, Bulawayo, 16th April, 1901 ; officer in charge customs, Plumtree, 1st October, 1901.

WATERMEYER, John Philip Fairbairn, B.A.—Called to bar, Middle Temple, June, 1885, and admitted advocate of supreme court of the Cape, July, 1885 ; appointed judge of the high court of Matabeleland, July, 1896.

WEBBER, Oliver Webb — Cape postal department, April, 1889 ; entered Rhodesian postal service as assistant, 12th May, 1896.

WESTLEY, CLARENCE HAROLD.— Postal assistant, New South Wales, 8th July, 1889 ; entered Cape service as telegraphist, April, 1897 ; entered Rhodesian service as telegraphist, 21st January, 1899 ; acting chief telegraphist, Salisbury, 26th September, 1901.

WILLIAMS, ALFRED GEORGE.— Junior assistant, Capetown office, 1st November, 1895 ; clerk, chief accountant's department, 15th March, 1898.

WILLIAMS, JAMES HERBERT.— Joined native department, 1st March, 1897 ; served through native rebellion with Victoria Volunteers, 1896-7 ; assistant native commissioner, Gutu's.

WOLHUTER, GEORGE HENRY.— Cape postal department, May, 1892 ; entered Rhodesian service as postal assistant, November, 1895 ; postmaster, 1st May, 1898 ; chief assistant, Bulawayo, 1st April 1900 : postmaster, Umtali, 1st October, 1900.

YATES, FRANK ALAN (L).—Clerk, general stores, 15th June, 1896 ; clerk to C.C., Umtali, 1st September, 1897.

SERVICES OF OFFICERS OF NORTH-EASTERN RHODESIA.

BEAUFORT, LEICESTER PAUL, M.A., B.C.L.— Barrister, Inner Temple, 1879; member London school board, 1888; government secretary and judicial commissioner, British North Borneo, 1889; received the Jubilee medal; governor and commander in chief of the colony of Labuan and of the state of North Borneo, 1895-1900; appointed judge of the high court, North-eastern Rhodesia, June, 1901.

BURROW, RICHARD.—Member of city council, Truro, Cornwall, from 1897 to 1900; local secretary, South Kensington science and art department, Truro, 1900; entered North-eastern Rhodesia service, January 4th, 1901, as clerk in secretary's department; assistant accountant, August 1st, 1901.

CHESNAYE, CHRISTIAN PUREFOY.— Joined B.B. police, 1891: Matabele war, 1893; Ngami Lake and Kalahari, 1894-95; joined M.M.P., 1896 rebellion (medal and clasp); sub-inspector and O.C. northern division, B.S.A. police, 1897-98: joined North-eastern Rhodesia service, July 4th, 1898; secretary to deputy administrator; secretary to administration; civil commissioner and magistrate, 1st August, 1900; acting secretary for native affairs, August,

1901; acting administrator and acting manager, A.T.T. Co., north of the Zambesi, October, 1901; justice of the peace.

CODRINGTON, HIS HONOUR, ROBERT EDWARD.— Joined B.B. police, 1890: Matabele war, 1893 (medal); joined Sir Harry Johnston's administration, British Central Africa, 1895; collector of revenues: received Central African medal: appointed deputy administrator, North-eastern Rhodesia, 1898; consular judicial officer, 1899; administrator, North-eastern Rhodesia, June, 1900; is also manager of the African transcontinental telegraph company, north of the Zambesi.

COOKSON, PERCY CHARLES.—Joined North-eastern Rhodesia service, December 24th, 1900; assistant native commissioner, 1st April, 1901: justice of the peace.

COXHEAD, JOHN CODRINGTON CHARLES. — Joined B.S.A. police, 1896; rebellion (medal); private secretary to deputy administrator, North-eastern Rhodesia, 1st June, 1898: native commissioner, 1st January, 1901: justice of the peace.

CROAD, HECTOR. —Joined British Central Africa administration, 1893;

appointed assistant collector, 1st January, 1894; native commissioner, 1st April, 1901 ; justice of the peace.

FORBES, James Hubert. — Appointed assistant collector, North eastern Rhodesia, August, 1896; native commissioner, 1st January, 1901; justice of the peace.

GOODE, Richard Allmond Jeffrey. —Special agent for B.S.A. Co. in Canada and United States, January, 1900 ; appointed to North-eastern Rhodesia, 1st July, 1900; secretary, North-eastern Rhodesia ; also acts as secretary of the African transcontinental telegraph company, north of Zambesi, and as registrar, North-eastern Rhodesia ; acting magistrate, May, 1901 ; justice of the peace.

GREER, John Lawrence.—Served three and half years in B.S.A. police ; appointed assistant collector, North-eastern Rhodesia, September, 1899 ; native commissioner, 1st January, 1901 ; justice of the peace.

HALL, Philip Edward, B.A., Oxford. —Joined North-eastern Rhodesia service, 11th January, 1901 ; assistant native commissioner, 1st April, 1901 ; justice of the peace.

HARRINGTON, Hubert Tyler.— Served in scouts, Matabele war, 1893 ; agent for B.S.A. Co., Beira railway, 1894 ; joined Northern Rhodesia police, 1st April, 1895; appointed assistant collector, 1st September, 1895 ; native commissioner, 1st January, 1901 ; justice of the peace.

JOHNSTONE, Berte Bromley.— Appointed assistant collector, North-eastern Rhodesia, 1st April, 1899 ; native commissioner, 1st January, 1901 ; justice of the peace.

JONES, Francis Emilius Fletcher. —Joined A.T.T. Co., April, 1897 ; assistant surveyor ; appointed assistant collector, North-eastern Rhodesia, 1st March, 1900 ; native commissioner, 1st January, 1901 ; justice of the peace.

JONES, Edgar Anderson Averay, B.A., Camb. — Joined North-eastern Rhodesia service, 4th July, 1901 ; appointed assistant native commissioner, 15th August, 1901.

KENNELLY, William Patrick.— Served in Cape mounted rifles ; three years in B.B.P. ; campaign, 1893 ; adjutant, Victoria column ; Shangani and Bembezi ; Rhodesia horse volunteers, 1895 ; campaign 1896, captain, Umtali rifles, commanding " A " and " C " squadrons ; joined A.T.T. Co. ; assistant constructor, 1897 ; appointed assistant collector, North-eastern Rhodesia, 1st January, 1900 ; native commissioner, 1st January, 1901 ; justice of the peace.

LEYER, George Magnus Ernest.— Served in B.B. police and B.S.A. police ; appointed assistant collector, North-eastern Rhodesia, 28th March, 1899 ; native commissioner, 1st January, 1901 ; justice of the peace.

MacDONALD, Robert Struthers. —Appointed clerk to civil commissioner and magistrate, Fife, December, 1900 ; assistant native commissioner, 1st January, 1901 ; justice of the peace.

McKINNON, Charles John.—Appointed collector, North-eastern Rhodesia, 1896 ; consular judicial officer, 1899 ; civil commissioner and magistrate, 1st August, 1900.

MARSHALL, Hugh Charlie. — Joined British Central Africa administration, 1891 ; consular judicial officer, 30th November, 1891 ; appointed collector, North-eastern Rhodesia, 1893 ; consular judicial officer, February, 1894 ; civil commissioner and magistrate, 1st August, 1900.

MELLAND, Frank Hulme, B.A., Oxford. — Joined North-eastern Rhodesia service, 4th July, 1901 ; appointed assistant native commissioner, 15th August, 1901.

MILLER, Adam Cook Robertson. —Appointed assistant collector, North-eastern Rhodesia, 10th April, 1897 ; native commissioner, 1st January, 1901 ; justice of the peace.

PARKIN, HENRY CLARENCE.—Joined North-eastern Rhodesia service, 24th April, 1899 ; clerk to secretary, 1st March, 1901.

SAVAGE, WALTER EDWIN METHUEN. —Joined A.T.T. Co., 1898 ; appointed assistant collector, North-eastern Rhodesia, 1st October, 1900 ; native commissioner, 1st January, 1901 ; justice of the peace.

SELBY, PHILIP HAMILTON.—Served in " D " troop, B.S.A. police, 1890-91 ; Joined A.T.T. Co., 1st June, 1897 ; in charge of transport north of Zambesi ; appointed collector, North-eastern Rhodesia, 1st July, 1898 ; civil commissioner and magistrate, 1st August, 1900.

SHEKLETON, CECIL COURTNEY.—Joined A.T.T. Co. 1st January, 1897 ; in charge of transport north of Zambesi, July, 1898 ; appointed to North-eastern Rhodesia service, 1st January, 1900 ; acting collector, February, 1900 ; native commissioner, 1st January, 1901 ; justice of the peace.

STEPHENSON, JOHN EDWARD.- Clerk, English posts and telegraphs, 1890-96 ; Cape government telegraphs, 15th August, 1896, to 31st May, 1897 ; Rhodesia telegraphs, June, 1897, to 31st March, 1898 ; A.T.T. Co., January, 1899, to 30th June, 1900 ; appointed assistant collector, North-eastern Rhodesia, 1st July, 1900 ; native commissioner, 1st January, 1901 ; justice of the peace.

STEVENS, CECIL.—Joined North-eastern Rhodesia service, 24th November, 1900 ; acting private secretary to administrator ; assistant native commissioner, 1st April, 1901 ; justice of the peace.

TAGART, EDWARD SAMUEL BOURN, B.A., Camb. — Joined North-eastern Rhodesia service, 11th January, 1901 ; assistant native commissioner, 1st April, 1901 ; justice of the peace.

TIMMLER, CLEMENT HENRY. — Cape civil service, 1893-98 ; appointed clerk to postmaster general, Salisbury, 1st April, 1898 ; transferred to mines and public works, July, 1898 ; acting chief accountant, North-eastern Rhodesia, 1st January, 1900 ; appointed chief clerk and distributor of stamps, North-eastern Rhodesia, 25th September, 1901.

WATSON, BLAIR, M.D.—Assistant collector and surgeon, British Central Africa administration, 1892 ; appointed collector, North-eastern Rhodesia, 1893 ; civil commissioner and magistrate, 1st August, 1900.

WILLIS, HENRY GRAHAM.—Joined North-eastern Rhodesia service, 18th October, 1900 ; assistant native commissioner, 1st January, 1901 ; justice of the peace.

YOUNG, ROBERT ANDREW.—Served two years in Mashonaland mounted police ; six months in Matabeleland mounted police ; appointed assistant collector, North-eastern Rhodesia, 1st May, 1895 ; native commissioner, 1st January, 1901 ; justice of the peace.

CIVIL SERVICE LAW EXAMINATION.

Through the courtesy of the University of the Cape of Good Hope, the Civil Servants of Rhodesia are admitted to the Law Examinations conducted by the University for the Civil Servants of the Cape Colony.

The attention of Civil Servants is drawn to Section 16 of the Civil Service of Rhodesia Regulations, 1898.

CIVIL SERVICE LAW EXAMINATIONS.

The subjects for the examination are as follows :—

(a) The Elements of Roman-Dutch Law : Van der Linden's *Institutes of the Law of Holland.* [Candidates are recommended to read Supreme Court Reports of cases bearing upon points of law and practice dealt with by the author.]

(b) The Elements of English Law (two papers) : Indermaur's *Principles of Common Law ;* Harris's *Principles of the Criminal Law,* omitting Book IV. (Summary Convictions.)

(c) Selections from Colonial Statute Law (two papers) : The following Ordinances and Acts of Parliament :—Ordinance 40 of 1828, Ordinance 73 of 1830, ~~Ordinance 2 of 1837,~~ Ordinance 8 of 1852, Act 3 of 1861, Act 15 of 1864, Act 7 of 1873, Act 17 of 1874, Act 13 of 1886, Act 20 of 1856, Act 12 of 1860, Act 12 of 1869, Act 21 of 1876, Act 43 of 1885, Act 1 of 1894, Act 21 of 1869, Act 7 of 1879, Act 8 of 1889, Act 4 of 1892, Act 38 of 1895, Act 15 of 1856, Act 18 of 1873, Act 7 of 1875, Ordinance 6 of 1843, ~~Ordinance 3 of 1844,~~ Act 38 of 1844, Act 35 of 1893, Act 21 of 1884, Act 17 of 1886, Act 12 of 1886, ~~Act 10 of 1900,~~ Act 8 of 1879.

EXAMINATION PAPERS, DECEMBER, 1901.

ROMAN-DUTCH LAW.

Time—Three Hours.

EXAMINER : Advocate KING, M.A.

1. *A* sells to *B* a carriage then in *A's* store for £50 cash and *B* arranges to send for it next day : in whom does the property in the carriage remain in the meantime ?

If the carriage were destroyed that night by an accidental fire, on whom would the loss fall?

Would it make any difference in either of these respects if the sale had been on credit?

2. Discuss whether and how far a sale can be legally cancelled (*a*) on account of deceit on the seller's part, (*b*) on its being subsequently discovered that the price paid was five times the real value of the article, (*c*) on a defect being found in the article sold which neither seller nor purchaser noticed at the time of sale.

3. What is meant by *novation* of a debt? and state fully its effects.

What are the requisites of *compensation* or *set off*?

4. *A* lets *B* a house for £20 a month, payable monthly, and no further express stipulations are made:

(1) Enumerate the duties of *A* and *B* respectively.

(2) If at the end of eighteen months *B* has paid no rent and is still in occupation, has *A* any advantages over *B's* other creditors?

5. On what grounds can a person be arrested? Describe the procedure.

6. In an ordinary partnership to carry on a business or trade for what debts are the partners liable?

What are partnerships *en commandite* and anonymous partnerships?

Do they differ from ordinary partnerships as to the liability of the partners?

7. *A* who owes *B* money gives him a written document pledging his two horses as security and hands over the two horses to *B*; *B* the same day lent the two horses to *A* to use in his business, and they remain with *A* till a week later when *X*, another creditor of *A's*, seizes the two horses under a writ of execution.

In an interpleader suit *A* and *X* claim the horses. State, with your reasons, which you consider entitled to them.

8. When suing for money due how do you determine from what date to claim interest?

Is there any limit to the rate of interest which can legally be agreed upon?

Is there any limit to the amount of interest which can be claimed in an action?

9. What is the difference between real and personal servitudes?

How are real servitudes acquired?

10. What are the rules with regard to (*a*) a married woman, (*b*) a minor suing in an action?

11. How does Van der Linden define the following crimes and what does he say as to the penalties?

High treason (*crimen perduellionis*); Treason (*crimen laesae Majestatis*); Sedition.

Give the substance of his remarks on *homicide in self-defence*.

ENGLISH LAW (FIRST PAPER).

Time—Three Hours.

EXAMINER: Mr. C. H. VAN ZYL.

1. What is the origin of the Common Law of England? and how is it distinguished from Equity?

2. Name the actions to which the maxim *Actio personalis moritur cum persona* applies, and those actions where it does not apply.

3. Define, and give examples of, Estoppel, Stoppage in Transitu, Son assault demesne, Quantum meruit, and Market-Overt.

4. What are the rules for the construction of Agreements, literary and verbal?

5. *A* and *B* domiciled in England enter into a contract there by which the latter is to act as a Mine-Manager in Johannesburg at a salary of a £100 per month. What Law and what Forum govern the contract? Give your reasons.

6. What is meant by the expression "*Consideration* for the agreement"? What agreements are valid without a consideration? What agreements are invalid because of the consideration therein mentioned?

7. What contracts must be in writing? and what contracts need not be in writing?

8. What are the duties, liabilities and obligations of landlords and tenants to each other, and for rates, taxes, tithes, assessments and repairs?

9. What is the meaning of the term Statutes of Limitation? and give the chief periods of limitation fixed by those statutes.

10 State the distinction between Torts and Crimes, and name those torts which amount to crimes, and those which do not.

ENGLISH LAW (SECOND PAPER).

Time—Three Hours.

EXAMINER : Mr. C. H. van ZYL.

1. Define and give examples of Felony, Misdemeanour, Larceny, Burglary, Poaching, and Penal-Servitude.

2. Who and under what circumstances are certain persons exempted from criminal responsibility? Give your reasons.

3. What constitutes Principals in the first and in the second degrees? and what constitutes Accessories before and after the fact? Give examples?

4. Give two examples of what amounts to Piracy, and two examples of what constitutes a levying of war.

5. Define and give three examples of what constitutes Overt-acts.

6. Give three examples of what amounts to Bribery at Parliamentary elections.

   (*a*) On the part of the Candidate ;
   (*b*) And two examples on the part of anyone else.

And if both are found guilty, state what punishments they are liable to, and what disabilities they are subject to.

7. Give two examples of what amounts to a Rout and to a Riot, and state what are the essentials of the latter.

8. Assume any two facts which will amount to Conspiracy, and state the gist of the offence.

9. Give examples of who can be prosecuted as Rogues and Vagabonds, and state the sentences that can be passed on them by the judge.

10. Give any two facts which will justify putting a person upon his trial for embezzlement, and distinguish Embezzlement from Larceny.

STATUTE LAW (FIRST PAPER).

Time—Three Hours.

EXAMINER : Advocate HOWEL JONES, B.A.

1. What jurisdiction has a Magistrate in actions for rent and for ejectment ?   Upon what principles should a Magistrate act when in an action for debt the defendant pleads a counter-claim the amount of which is beyond his jurisdiction ?

2. What is meant by a return of *nulla bona* ?   Where such a return has been made in answer to a writ of execution issued out of a Magistrate's Court, what are the various remedies which the creditor may avail himself of (*a*) if the debtor remains within the original magisterial jurisdiction and (*b*) if he removes into another district ?

3. A person has evidence that a female servant recently in his employment has committed a theft of his property.   Describe in detail the steps which must be taken in order to have her arrested and brought to trial in a Magistrate's Court.   In the event of her guilt being proved what sentence may the Magistrate impose summarily ?   What further duty is imposed upon the Magistrate after passing sentence ?

4. What are the powers given by the Statute Law to the Attorney-General with respect to criminal prosecutions ;   What are the conditions and the procedure necessary before a private prosecution can be instituted ?

5. State the proceedings necessary between the arrest of a prisoner and his trial before a jury and the limits of time within which such proceedings must respectively be taken.

After service of an indictment can the trial be postponed ?   If so, at what period of the proceedings, upon what grounds and upon what conditions may this be done ?

6.   Mention the provisions of Act 3 of 1861 with respect to allegations and proof of previous convictions.

7. What sentences is a Magistrate empowered to impose specially in the case of juvenile offenders ?   Is he compelled to draw any distinction between male and female offenders of this class ?

8. Mention the provisions of the Statute Law as to the class of witnesses who

    (*a*) must be sworn,
    (*b*) may affirm,
    (*c*) must be admonished to speak the truth.

What are the questions which a Magistrate should put to a witness when it appears necessary to examine him touching his knowledge of the obligation of an oath.

9. Draw the form of plaint required to be entered in a Magistrate's Civil Record Book where the plaintiff claims

    (*a*) the purchase price of a horse sold by him,
    (*b*) damages sustained through being knocked down owing to the
        defendant's careless driving,
    (*c*) damages for breaking down his dam.

10. What is the Magistrate's Court procedure
    (*a*) where the plaintiff is in default,
    (*b*) where the defendant is in default ?

Under what circumstances may the case be reopened?

Who has to pay the costs in each of these cases?

STATUTE LAW (SECOND PAPER).

Time—Three Hours.

EXAMINER: Advocate JOUBERT, B.A., LL.B.

1. What tacit Hypothecations are abolished by Act 5 of 1861?

2. To what suits or actions does the eight years period of prescription apply?

What is the effect of an acknowledgment of debt or promise to pay, in taking any cause of action out of the operation of the Prescription Act No. 6 of 1861?

Supposing a cause of action arises against two joint debtors, one of whom is absent from the Colony;—how is the creditor to enforce his claim if he wishes to prevent prescription?

3. What is the presumption as to the period for which a contract of service is entered into, in case the term of endurance shall not be specially expressed? What exceptions are there to the rule?

For how long are (a) verbal and (b) written contracts of service valid?

4. What are the offences mentioned in Section 7 of Act 18 of 1873 for which servants or apprentices not under 16 can be punished? What penalty may be imposed? To what class of servants and apprentices does the section apply?

5. Define and explain the nature and limitations of the following tacit hypothecs, viz.:

(a) Of Government for arrear rent or taxes.

(b) Of minors on the estates of their guardians.

(c) Of legatees in security for their legacies.

6. What persons are disqualified from being trustees in insolvent estates?

What are the grounds on which the office of trustee is forfeited?

7. (a) What is provided by Section 83 of the Insolvent Ordinance as to the alienation of property by an insolvent at a time when his liabilities fairly valued exceed his assets fairly valued?

(b) What is the law as to alienations by an insolvent to a creditor in the usual and ordinary course of business?

8. State fully the provisions of the Insolvent Ordinance as to the proof of debts on an insolvent estate by creditors whose debts depend upon a contingency or an uncertain condition.

9. Act 38 of 1884 repeals the Insolvents' Rehabilitation Act No. 15 of 1859, and re-enacts Section 117 of Ordinance 6 of 1843 with certain amendments. What was enacted by that section of the Ordinance and what are the provisos added by the Act of 1881?

10. What are the provisions of the Masters and Servants Acts with regard to characters given by masters to their servants or apprentices?

THE FOLLOWING IS A LIST OF SUCCESSFUL RHODESIAN CANDIDATES:

1898.—W. S. Taberer.

1899. (June Examination.)

E. J. Lawlor.
T. B. Hulley..
G. McCulloch.

1899. (December Examination.)

A. E. Speight.
H. M. G. Jackson.
A. Drew.
C. T. Stuart.
A. A. Campbell.

1900. (June Examination.)

G. M. Huntly.
S. N. G. Jackson.
M. W. Barnard.
F. A. Yates.
W. E. Thomas.
H. H. A. De Laessoe.
J. T. Fisher.
C. M. Fletcher.
T. M. Thomas.
R. A. Blanckenberg.
L L. Bayne.
P. A. Stuart.

1900. (December Examination.)

C. J. R. Gardiner.
H. Rangeley.
W R. Blanckenberg.
F. J. Clarke.
R. Lanning.
F. W. Sykes.
C. W. Cary.

www.ingramcontent.com/pod-product-compliance
Lightning Source LLC
Chambersburg PA
CBHW051813040426
42446CB00007B/649